Skip·Beat!

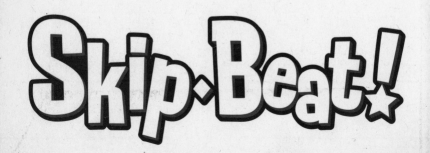

Shojo Beat

Skip·Beat!

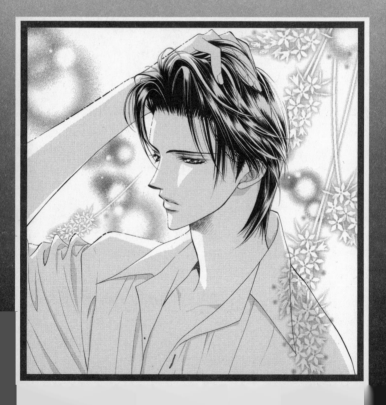

Skip·Beat!

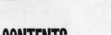

Volume 6

CONTENTS

Skip·Beat!

Act 30: The Secret Stamp Book

SECTION
SECTION

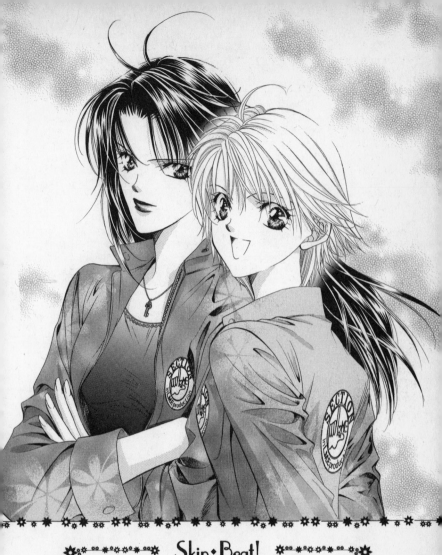

Skip·Beat!

6

After the results of the commercial audition were announced.
I WANT YOU GUYS TO BE VERY CARE-FUL...
...ABOUT TWO THINGS. DON'T GET SICK OR HURT YOURSELF UNTIL THE SHOOTING IS OVER.
MAKE SURE THAT YOU'RE IN YOUR BEST FORM TO MAINTAIN YOUR BEAUTY AND HEALTH.
YOU HAVE TO DO THIS NATURALLY, JUST LIKE YOU BREATHE. THIS IS AN OBLIGATION THAT YOU HAVE TO FULFILL.

THAT'S BE-CAUSE...
...EVEN IF YOU ARE A NEWCOMER, OR A NO-NAME, ONCE YOU'RE GETTING PAID TO DO WORK, YOU'RE A PROFESSIONAL.
Your body doesn't only belong to you anymore.
YOUR BODY IS YOUR TOOL FOR THIS BUSI-NESS...
...AND ANYBODY WHO CAN'T MAINTAIN THAT LACKS PROFES-SIONALISM.

AND ...
...I HATE ...
... PEOPLE WHO AREN'T PROFES-SIONAL.
HYUOOOO
DO YOU UNDER-STAND ?
THIS IS NOT A THREAT.
.....
IF YOU HURT YOURSELF EVEN A LITTLE BEFORE THE SHOOTING IS OVER...
...EVEN IF THE SHOOTING ISN'T OVER YET...
.....

...I'LL FIRE YOU ON THE SPOT, NO MERCY!
Do you under-stand?!
THIS ALWAYS HAPPENS... I WISH HE WOULDN'T MAKE THESE DECISIONS HIMSELF...
WE'RE THE ONE SIGNING THE CONTRACTS...
Y-Yes!!
H-HE'S SCARY!
He IS a low-rank yakuza...
....
DID YOU HEAR THAT?
YES.
THIS IS AN OPPORTUNITY FOR A COMEBACK.
Eavesdropping
WE'RE GOING TO TAKE ADVANTAGE OF THE DIRECTOR'S TEMPER, RIGHT?
EXACTLY.

IF KANAE KOTONAMI GETS SICK OR IS INJURED, SHE'LL BE FIRED!
THEN MS. ERIKA WILL PROBABLY BE MOVED UP AND APPEAR IN THE COMMERCIAL!
YES.
I STILL HAVE A CHANCE TO CRUSH HER DREAM OF GETTING UNDER THE SPOTLIGHT!
hmph
Wonderful~!!
clap clap clap
clap
clap
clap
THAT'S OUR MS. ERIKA! YOU NEVER GIVE UP UNTIL THE VERY END!
I WILL NOT FORGIVE YOU...
...KANAE KOTONAMI!
DEFEATING ME NOT ONCE, BUT TWICE!
MOREOVER, THIS TIME SHE DID IT TO SPITE ME!
SHE SMILED SUCH A TRIUMPHANT SMILE, LIKE SHE WAS MORE TALENTED THAN ME!
grin

DON'T THINK THAT YOU CAN GET AWAY WITH IT!
DO YOU HEAR ME?
CRUSH KANAE KOTONAMI, NO MATTER WHAT YOU HAVE TO DO!
YES, MS. ERIKA!
I...
...WILL MAKE SURE THAT YOU CAN NEVER DREAM OF BECOMING AN ACT-RESS, EVER!
THANK YOU SO MUCH!
Yes.
THANK YOU. TAKE CARE.
BOW
BOW
...
WE'LL DISCUSS THE DETAILS ABOUT THE COMMERCIAL AT THE NEXT MEETING.
YES.
....
MS. MOGAMI.
YES?
WHAT WAS IT?

WHAT?
THE DIRECTOR.
clip clop clip
clip clop
OH.
NOTHING MUCH...
HE ASKED ABOUT THE CURARA I USED IN THE SECOND ROUTINE OF THE AUDITION.
HE ASKED ME WHY I'D USED THE CAN AND GAVE YOU THE PLASTIC BOTTLE ON PURPOSE.
AND...
...IF I'D KNOWN THAT THE DRINK FROM THE BOTTLE WOULDN'T SPURT AS MUCH AS THE CAN.
!!
SHE HAD IT...
I WONDER WHY HE ASKED ME THAT?
...IN A FLASH!
...ALL FIGURED OUT...
THAT'S TRUE...
Yaaaaa!
She's lost her cool.
Bwa!
YES...IF I'D BEEN HOLDING THE CAN INSTEAD...
...THINGS...
...WOULDN'T HAVE GONE SO SMOOTHLY.
MOKO, YOU KNEW THAT SODA IN PLASTIC BOTTLES SPURTS OUT LIKE THAT, RIGHT?

Digression

I liked Ruby's idea of Yanki fashion quite a bit when it was first printed in the magazine. But not as much as drawing it in the sidebar now...

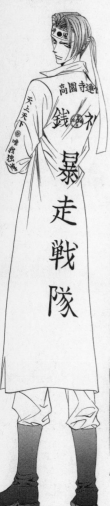

天上天下
暴走戦隊

THIS GIRL!
...
She thought that it would spurt out just like from the can, so she was really surprised.
She doesn't drink soda for health reasons.
O-OH?
SHE'S ...
...A TOUGH ONE...
HUH?
DID YOU SAY SOMETHING?
NO...
Nothing.
clip clop
clip clop
clip clop
clip clop
clip clop
IN ANY CASE, I'M LOOKING FORWARD TO THIS COMMERCIAL.
PEOPLE SAY THAT TALENTOS WHO APPEAR IN KAINDO'S COMMERCIALS ALWAYS BECOME POPULAR...
...AND THAT'LL BE THE CASE THIS TIME, TOO.

MS. KOTONAMI ESPECIALLY IS PRETTY BEAUTIFUL, AND SHE CAN ACT GREAT...
...SHE'S GUARANTEED TO SELL WELL.
YEAH.
...HOWEVER...
Those two really acted well.
happy happy
I'm really looking forward to having the two appear in our commercial, and wowing the whole world.
SURE...
...THAT MAY BE THE CASE WITH KANAE KOTONAMI...
...THAT GIRL...
...WHO BLEW ERIKA KOENJI TO PIECES, WHEN SHE WAS ONE OF THE LEADING CANDIDATES UNTIL THE VERY END.
I CAN'T KEEP...
...MY EYES OFF OF HER.
ACTUALLY, I REALLY DON'T LIKE SODA...
...I DON'T DRINK IT MYSELF...
...SO WHENEVER I HAPPENED TO DRINK IT, I ALWAYS SHOOK IT, AND MADE A MESS.
UHYAAAA
SPLOOSH
drib drib
And sometimes the drink spilled on her.

...
WHY'D YOU "HAPPEN TO DRINK IT" IF YOU DON'T LIKE IT?
You just don't have to drink it.
Kyoko, good job. Here, drink this.
Shotaro's mom.
BUT AFTER WORK, THE OKAMISAN USED TO GIVE IT TO ME, SO I COULDN'T REFUSE.
Because I was so noble.
OKAMISAN?
OOPS
OH NO! I WAS ABOUT TO SPILL MY SECRET!
How careless of me!
U-UM, THE OKAMISAN OF THE PLACE I'M WORKING AT...
HMPH.
hiding
....
Hmph.
BECAUSE SHE WON THE AUDITION, SHE'S COMPLETELY OFF GUARD.
Now's the time.
ARE YOU READY ...
...YOU GUYS?!
YES, MS. ERIKA!
whapoo———!
Emerald Sakazaki
Sapphire Todo
Ruby Hojo
EACH GUY'S IDEA OF YANKI FASHION.

YOU UNDERSTAND WHAT YOU'RE SUPPOSED TO DO?
Yes.
WE BUMP INTO KANAE KOTONAMI.
WE TELL HER TO COMPENSATE US FOR A BROKEN BONE.
IF SHE WON'T PAY, WE INJURE HER SO THAT SHE TAKES A MONTH TO RECOVER!
Yes!
TARGET HER FACE, WHICH IS AN ACTRESS' MAIN ASSET!
A traditional method handed down from ancient times.
GO!
YES, MISS!
DASH
HUH?
THIS IS THE FIRST TIME...
excited
...I'VE WALKED IN TOWN WITH A FEMALE FRIEND.
.....
HEY ... MOKO ...
...DO YOU OFTEN COME TO TOWN WITH YOUR FRIENDS?
....
WHY?
GIRLS DIDN'T LIKE ME.
Every girl in school hated me.
MATTER-OF-FACT

NO... ALL THE GIRLS IN THE DIS-TRICT?
Because of the live concerts, Shotaro's fans were increasing all the time.
hmm
SHE'S REALLY LIKE ME.
Me... and her...
...
SH-
sneak
ALL RIGHT, WE'LL DO IT.
YEAH.
CASUALLY, BUT WITH A FORCE THAT COULD BREAK A BONE!
This is for Ms. Erika!
Right!
TROMP TROMP TROMP TROMP
Moko, Look at THAT!
SHPROIN
OH.
OH NO!
G
BUMP
HUH?!
GLARE
WHA?

OUCH!
YOU ALL RIGHT, TEC-CHIN?
shuf
EEP!
YOU DORK, WATCH WHERE YOU'RE WALKING!
MY BONE'S BROKEN, PAY UP!
RAAAAAAH!
AAAAAAH!
THUNK
SMACK
Hey, hey.
This is so cute! ♡
It'll really look good on you, Moko!
REAAALLY?
It's not my style.
SILENCE...
... ...
I mean...
THAT'S HOW FEMALE FRIENDS TALK, RIGHT?
WHERE DID YOU HEAR THAT?!
GIRLS WHO TALK LIKE THAT ARE ONLY PRETENDING TO BE FRIENDS.
worn out
limp limp
wheeze
Th-That was Bad...
Darn... we'll get you the next time...
MO NO NO!!
AHHH!
YOU HAVE TO SAY
Huh?
WHAT THE HECK?
WHEN GIRLS GET TOGETHER, THEY ONLY ENJOY BAD-MOUTHING OTHER GIRLS.
No NO!
Don't say things that shatter my dreams!
IT'S TRUE!

THAT'S WHY...
...I...
...DON'T LIKE TO HUDDLE WITH OTHER PEOPLE...
....
MOKO...
DO YOUR FRIENDS SAY TERRIBLE THINGS BEHIND YOUR BACK?
Why don't you get rid of friends like that?
They're NOT friends!
They're like flies or mosquitoes to me!
GAH!
huh?
OH...
...THEN... YOU HAVEN'T HAD A GOOD FRIEND EITHER, MOKO.
uhh...
WH-WHAT? YOU GOTTA PROBLEM WITH THAT?!
NO.
I'M GLAD.
WHAT?!
...
sneak
...
sneak

...THEN I'M YOUR FIRST BEST FRIEND, MOKO! ♡

CUZ...

"WHO'S MY BEST FRIEND?"

sneak sneak

Ready!

All right, now!

"DON'T AS-SUME THAT YOU ARE."

MOKO! LOOK LOOK! COME WITH MEEEE!

Kyaaaaaaaa

TOPPLE

Oops!

Oops!

Oops!

SHA

BOOM

FWOSH

OH.

AAHHHHHHHHH!
roll roll roll roll roll
What is it THIS time?!
"I...
...DON'T WANT TO BE INVOLVED IN A BOTHERSOME RELATIONSHIP LIKE BEST FRIENDS."
......
I WONDER WHY I CAN'T SAY IT.
Honestly, like always.
I COULD SAY IT UNTIL YESTERDAY...
Why didn't you say something like that at least?!
You ignored me! You ignored me again!
Moko, you fool! How can you do this?! You're so mean! I'm going to get real angry today!
Shut up! Mo—!
WHO'S YOUR BEST FRIEND?!
Don't make ME your best friend!
I DECIDED THAT I WON'T TALK TO YOU!
GRAB
Blah blah blah
Blah blah
excited
Kyoko treated her.
I'VE ALWAYS WANTED TO EAT THIS...
..."WITH A FRIEND ON THE WAY HOME."
NOT ONLY THAT...
...JUST A WHILE BACK...

...IF I'D KNOWN THAT THE DRINK FROM THE BOTTLE WOULDN'T SPURT AS MUCH AS THE CAN.
!!
...I WAS ON GUARD ...
...
THIS GIRL!
SHE'S SOMEONE TO WATCH OUT FOR...
O-OH?
...BUT...
YOU'RE MY RIVAL!
...I DIDN'T FEEL LIKE PUSHING HER AWAY.
THE REASON ...
...
... FOR THAT IS...
M-MS. ERIKA.
THAT POVERTY-STRICKEN GIRL IS NO ORDINARY GIRL!
SHE MUST HAVE SUPERNATURAL POWERS, OR HAVE EYES IN THE BACK OF HER HEAD!
How can THAT be?!
What are you talking about?!
BECAUSE SHE PROTECTS KANAE KOTONAMI JUST AS WE'RE ABOUT TO GET HER.
AND WE ALWAYS GET HURT INDIRECTLY.
THERE MUST BE SOME UNNATURAL FORCES AT WORK!
Stupid!
ENOUGH! I'LL do it myself!
No!

N-No, Ms. Erika!
It's dangerous!
splish
splash
Ah.
THAT WAS DELICIOUS.
THE ICE CREAM!
happy
YES, REALLY.
IT WAS SO DELICIOUS, I HATED IT.
SO I ATE IT ALL.
When I know it's Bad for me.
WHY COULDN'T I STOP EATING AFTER ONE BITE?!
I'm usually not tempted By food!
Darn, what sort of cheeky taste did it...
EATING SOMETHING WITH SOMEBODY IS FUN.
THAT...
...MUST BE THE MAGIC...
THE MORE YOU "REALLY LIKE" TO BE WITH SOMEONE...
...THE MORE DELICIOUS SOMETHING TASTES.

Oh, this is like a confession of Loooove!
I can't Beliiiieve I said I liiiike Moko!!
KYAAAAAAA!
Have my feelings of love been resurrected?!
BOO-SH
SPLA—SH!
drip
drip
drip
drip
....
spleeeesh
splooosh
....
....

M-MS. KOENJI?
Oh... Ms. Erika, you were hurt too!
wheeze
hobble
WHAT'RE YOU DOING?
SPLOOSH
SHUNK
And the momentum made her fall into the fountain.
....
KANAE KOTONAMI.
MAKING ME ACT LIKE A FOOL...
CREAK
HUH? WHAT'RE YOU TALKING ABOUT?
Don't think you can escape so easily!
HURL
Wh—
WHAT'S GOING ON?!
AHHHH!
OOPS.
Oh no.
MS. ERIKA!
We have her!
KLONK
MOKO!

I HEARD ...
...THAT IF YOU'RE INJURED ...
...YOU'RE FIRED?
!!
IF..
...I HIT YOUR FACE WITH THIS, WILL IT SCAR YOUR FACE?
WILL IT?
....
YOU LOST BECAUSE YOU WEREN'T GOOD ENOUGH.
SO NOW YOU RESORT TO VIOLENCE ?!
YOU'RE ALWAYS THAT WAY.

WHY DON'T YOU UNDERSTAND THAT YOUR ATTITUDE IS THE REASON WHY YOU DON'T GET BETTER ?!
YOU ...
...ALWAYS DEPEND ON YOUR MONEY TO BAIL YOU OUT.
SLAMMING AGAINST WHAT SEEMS IMPOSSIBLE UNTIL YOU FALL TO PIECES...
WHEN YOU FOUND OUT WHAT YOUR LIMITS WERE...
...HAVE YOU EVER HAD TO DO EVERY-THING YOU POSSIBLY COULD?
YOU'VE NEVER DONE IT...
NOT EVEN ONCE!
MOKO...

.....
YOU...
...ARE STANDING IN A PEACEFUL AND BEAUTIFUL WORLD...
...WHERE YOU NEVER FALL DOWN AND GET COVERED IN MUD, EVEN IF YOU TRIP.
YOU...
...ARE STANDING IN A WORLD THAT'S DIFFERENT FROM MINE.
BE- CAUSE ...
...WE'RE STANDING ON DIFFERENT FIELDS...
...THERE'S NO COMPETING!
IF YOU WANT TO BEAT ME...
...STEP DOWN FROM YOUR WORLD.
AND GET COVERED IN MUD YOUR- SELF.
THEN ...
BING
BONG
...THEN...

BING
...I...
...WILL CALL YOU MY RIVAL...
BONG
BONG
BING
...
mumble
... WON'T FORGIVE YOU...
... FOR ...
... LECTURING ME LIKE THAT...

I'LL...
...MAKE YOU REGRET ...
...THAT YOU EVER SAID...
... "STEP DOWN"!
THEN...
TO GET WHAT YOU WANT...
...YOU'VE GOT TO FIGHT.

...YOU'VE GOT TO BE WILLING TO GET COVERED IN MUD...
I'LL BE WAITING FOR YOU.
VROOOO
VROOOM
VROOM
MOKO...
...just then...
...you were soooo cool!
sparkle
THAT'S WHY I'M EVEN MORE OVERWHELMED.
yeeees.
YOU USED MY WORDS, MOKO...
...BECAUSE THEY BURNED IN FIERCELY YOUR HEART, RIGHT?
I'm telling you not to look at me with those eyes!
TH-THAT...
...WAS JUST WHAT SOMEBODY SAID.
When she puts it that way, I don't want to admit it...
I'M REALLY HAPPY ABOUT THAT...

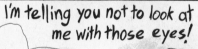

... CUZ...
...THAT'S REALLY LIKE...
...KINDA BEING A BEST FRIEND, RIGHT?
"KINDA" ?
URK
WHAT DO YOU MEAN, "KINDA" ?
HEY.
YOU JUST DECLARED YOURSELF MY FIRST BEST FRIEND, DIDN'T YOU?!
UH.
ZZZ—
snorre
wonk wonk
SHE'S ASLEEP?!

HEY! YOU FALL FAST ASLEEP AND LEAVE ME ALONE?!
And in just three seconds?! That's too quick!
Pyoo-yoro-fu...
She can cry in three seconds.
How irre-spon-sible!
THAT'S HOW YOU ACT TOWARDS THE FIRST BEST FRIEND IN YOUR LIFE?!
huh?
...CONSID-ERING HER MY BEST FRIEND, TOO...
ha ha
...DEAR...
OH...
.....
blu~sh
MOOKOOO.
I'm ...

Let's ...

...do our best...

....

heh

zzz

MOKO...

...YOU WANT TO BE AN ACTRESS, RIGHT?

...IF...

THEN ...

I...

...YOU'VE GOT TO FIGHT ...

...MAY HAVE ONLY TRIED TO FIND A SMALL EXIT...

...I HADN'T...

...MET HER...

...STARTED...

...REACHING OUT FOR MY DREAM...

I'VE...

ponk

I believe today is a day that I will remember for the rest of my life. Let's do our best in the commercial, so that it will be a step towards our future.
Thank you.
Kanae Kotonami
Full Marks 100% Great Job
Full Marks 100% Great Job
THANK YOU...
...TO THE PARTNER I CAN TRUST...
End of Act 30

Skip·Beat!

Act 31: Together in the Minefield

ZSS————h

ZSS————h

AH...

OH... MR. YASHIRO, YOU'VE GOT A COLD?

AH...

...HOO!

HMM...

...MAY-BE.

WHEN I WENT TO THE OFFICE YESTERDAY, A LOT OF PEOPLE HAD COLDS...
...SO I MAY HAVE CAUGHT IT THERE.
I haven't been feeling well since this morning...
All right, cut!
Okay.
WHAT? THAT'S TERRIBLE.
You all right?
MR. YASHIRO.
DON'T GIVE YOUR COLD TO TSURUGA, ALL RIGHT?
Please.
I UNDERSTAND.
Yes, really...
MR. YASHIRO.
kssh kssh
ARE YOU ALL RIGHT?
YOU SHOULD HAVE SAT DOWN AND RESTED...
NO... IT'S NOT THAT BAD YET...
REALLY?
THEN CAN YOU EAT?
WE'RE HAVING LUNCH NOW.
Please come get your lunch box!
Ohh, food food!
Um.
YEAH, SURE.
UM.

UH, IF YOU DON'T MIND...
...MAY I EAT WITH YOU, TOO?
OF COURSE YOU MAY.
HYUU
OH.
OH?
SURE, LET'S EAT TOGETHER.
SMILE
I BROUGHT PLENTY OF DESSERT. ♡
SO I REALLY WANT YOU TO...
...HAVE SOME TOO! ♡
POP!
Skitter
Skitter
Skitter
Skitter
!!!!

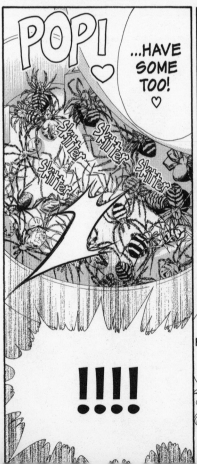

GYAAAA!
Noooooooo! That's gross!
FLE—E!!
HMPH.
evil grin
DON'T YOU EVER GET TOO CLOSE TO REN, YOU OLD WOMAN!
...
NYA
ha
click
YOUR VISION MUST BE GOING IN YOUR OLD AGE, CUZ YOU CAN'T EVEN TELL THAT THESE SPIDERS ARE FAKE!
REN...
...YOU... MIGHT END UP BEING SINGLE FOREVER...
I can't help but cry when I think about your future...
WHEN YOU'VE GOT A GIRLFRIEND, THIS LITTLE DEVIL WITH AN ANGEL'S FACE IS GOING TO TOTALLY BULLY HER...
tears
HI MARIA.
REN! ♡
You've really got something today.
I feel a little sorry for her...
Eeee!♡
LONG TIME NO SEEEE! ♡
I missed yoooooou! ♡
Yes, long time no see.
Purr purr purr
Ee hee
Ren, you smell good like always. ♡♡
MARIA, YOU CAME HERE ALONE?

I'M...
NO.
...HERE WITH MY GUARDIAN.
DA DA DA DA DU
Wah!
EEK!
IN
DA DA DA DA DU—N
Rata tat tat
Boomp Boomp
Wha ...
kkksssssshhhhhh
What, what ?!
Who are these people ?!
...
DUN DUN DUN DA
When did they get here ?!
And from where?!
H...
DUN DUN DA DA I H
!
DUN DUN DUN DAH
HE'S HERE.
heh
DUN DUN DUN DAH
DUN DUN DA I H
CLOP clop clop clop

LORY'S MAJE
FLAP
DODOOM
NEHEEY
HEY, REN.
LONG TIME NO SEE.
You doing your job?
eee
President...
As usual...
...YOU MAKE A GRAND ENTRANCE ...

DUN DUN DUN DAH DAH
DUN DUN DUN DAH DAH DOO DOO
Marching Song of Retreat
WH- WHAT IS THAT?
THEY WERE SAYING THAT THE LME PRESIDENT WAS HERE.
AH...
THE ONE WHO'S RUMORED TO BE... WEIRD...
AND...
...WHY DID THE LME PRESIDENT COME HERE?
Don't know.
WELL...
...I JUST DROPPED BY...
...TO SEE HOW THINGS WERE GOING.
WITH OUR DRAMA?
NO.
WE JUST STOPPED HERE ON OUR WAY.
BE-CAUSE MARIA INSIS-TED.
BECAUSE WHEN I FOUND OUT THAT YOU WERE HERE, REN, I COULDN'T PASS BY WITH-OUT SEEING YOU.
I can't resist the trap of love!
ON YOUR WAY...?
Cuz I'm a woman.
WHERE WERE YOU GOING?

Lory's Name

I wrote before that there is a reason why Lory's name is spelled in Japanese with a small "i" at the end instead of with a dash. The reason is this.

Lory Bird
↑
This is a name that only we call it by.

This bird is called Lory (depending on the type of bird, there seem to be names like Swainson's Lories and Rainbow Lory...)...anyway this Lory bird (called Rainbow above) is tropically colorful...so much...that you're greedy for using so many colors just by yourself... ♪ ...the one I used as a model was about five colors... ♪ ...So Lory Takarada's name comes from the Lory bird. The reason Lory's costumes always make my assistants cry is also because the Lory bird is a colorful, showy bird.

UM... UM...
TMP
...HER FIRST JOB...
...THE COMMERCIAL IS ABOUT TO FINISH SHOOTING TODAY!
SO I ARRANGED A SECRET PARTY AND CAME TO GET HER!
M-MARIA, YOU DID?
SHE'S DOING ALL THIS FOR SOMEONE OTHER THAN REN?!
Who is it for ?!
SHOOTING OF A COMMERCIAL... WHO'S DOING IT?

KYOKO! ♡

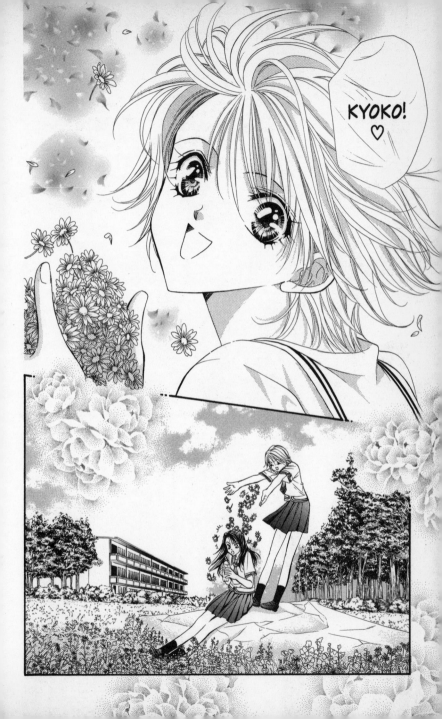

Yeee——e!
I'M SURPRISED.
KYOKO.
Oh, A-ko is chasing her.
SHE REALLY WON THAT AUDITION.
The Love Me pair did it.
....
WOW, WOW.
YES, SHE'S AMAZING. SHE WAS GREAT AT THE TRAINING SCHOOL, TOO!
She was so cool!

TRAIN-
ING
SCHOOL
?

"ACT-
RESS"...

YES. ♡
LME'S
TRAINING
SCHOOL FOR
ACTORS.

I became
friends
with her
there.

All
right.

Okay!

Kaaa!
↑
Cut

.....

THE
REASON I
BECAME
FRIENDS
WITH HER
IS...

You romped well!
Good job!
You guys are all done!
FWUMP
EXHAUSTED
huff huff
wheeze
huff huff huff
I-I'M EXHAUST-ED...
MO—!
HOW MANY TIMES DID WE "ROMP AROUND NATURALLY" ...?
Ah ha ha ha.
BUT I ACTUALLY ENJOYED IT.
It was fun.
sigh
YOU'RE...
... REALLY TOUGH.
toot
HUH?
SHA—!
chak
chak
chak
chak
?!
?!
URK
WH-WHO are THESE people?!
Wh-When did they get here?!
And from where?!

DUN DUN DAH DAH
DAH DAH DAH DUN
Ahhhh! Wh-What, what?!
PRESIDENT...
....
...HE HAS TO DO IT HERE, TOO...
IT'S HIS STYLE...
...
DADUN— DUN DUN DAH DUN— Bomp Bomp
NEHEY
Watch the equipment.
Blah
Blah
Blah
Oh.
That's a good horse.
munch
munch
munch
WELL...
...WE GOT GOOD SHOTS...
...SO NOW THE COMMERCIAL DEPENDS ON WHAT I DO...
...BUT DON'T WORRY.
I'M CONFIDENT ABOUT SELLING THE PRODUCT AND YOU GUYS.

WHEN THE TAPE'S READY, I'LL CONTACT YOUR AGENCY...
...SO LOOK FORWARD TO IT.
YES! YES!
Thank you!
Thank you!
Yeah, good job!
!
Kyoko!
Maria!
What're you doing here?
MR. KURO-SAKI.
THANK YOU FOR TAKING CARE OF OUR GIRLS.
bling bling
huge grin
uhhh...
NO...
sha
Well...
...thank you...
WOW...HEY, HEY, A GUY LIKE THIS IS REALLY THE PRESIDENT OF LME?
I'VE HEARD RUMORS ABOUT HIM, BUT...
I'VE HEARD RUMORS ABOUT YOU, BUT...
...YOU'VE GOT AN ORIGINAL STYLE, JUST AS I'VE HEARD.
No, you don't look like a director at all.
hah hah hah
I DON'T WANT YOU TALKING ABOUT MY "ORIGINAL STYLE."

HOW-EVER...
...YOUR PAST WORK...
...PROVES...
...YOUR TALENT.
....
I PRIDE MYSELF ON IT.
heh
THAT'S WHY...
...I WANTED TO MEET YOU...
WHAT?
kssh
MR. TSURUGA?
WAS HERE?
UH HUH.
The crew gave them the drinks.
HE WAS HERE JUST FOR A SHORT WHILE, DURING LUNCH BREAK...
...SO HE RETURNED TO THE SHOOTING RIGHT AWAY.
Lory's car, which took Ren and Yashiro back to the shooting.
Wow... a stretch limo that I've only ever seen on TV!
Don't get close to it. If you scratch it, you'll be forced to commit harakiri!

OH...
THEN...
...I DON'T HAVE TO TELL HIM I GOT THIS JOB.
I DIDN'T HAVE THE CHANCE TO MEET HIM, SO I COULDN'T TELL HIM.
.....
OH...
sip
WHAT'S THIS "OH"?!
Questioning herself.
HUH?
What?
...AND I THINK IT'S PROPER MANNERS TO TELL HIM DIRECTLY!
NO! I DIDN'T WANT TO SEE HIM!
BUT, BUT... HE CHEERED ME ON...
shup
NO, DEFINITELY!
KYOKO?
Answering herself.
Am I saying something wrong?
stare
???
N-No.
She forces her to agree.
SHOOM

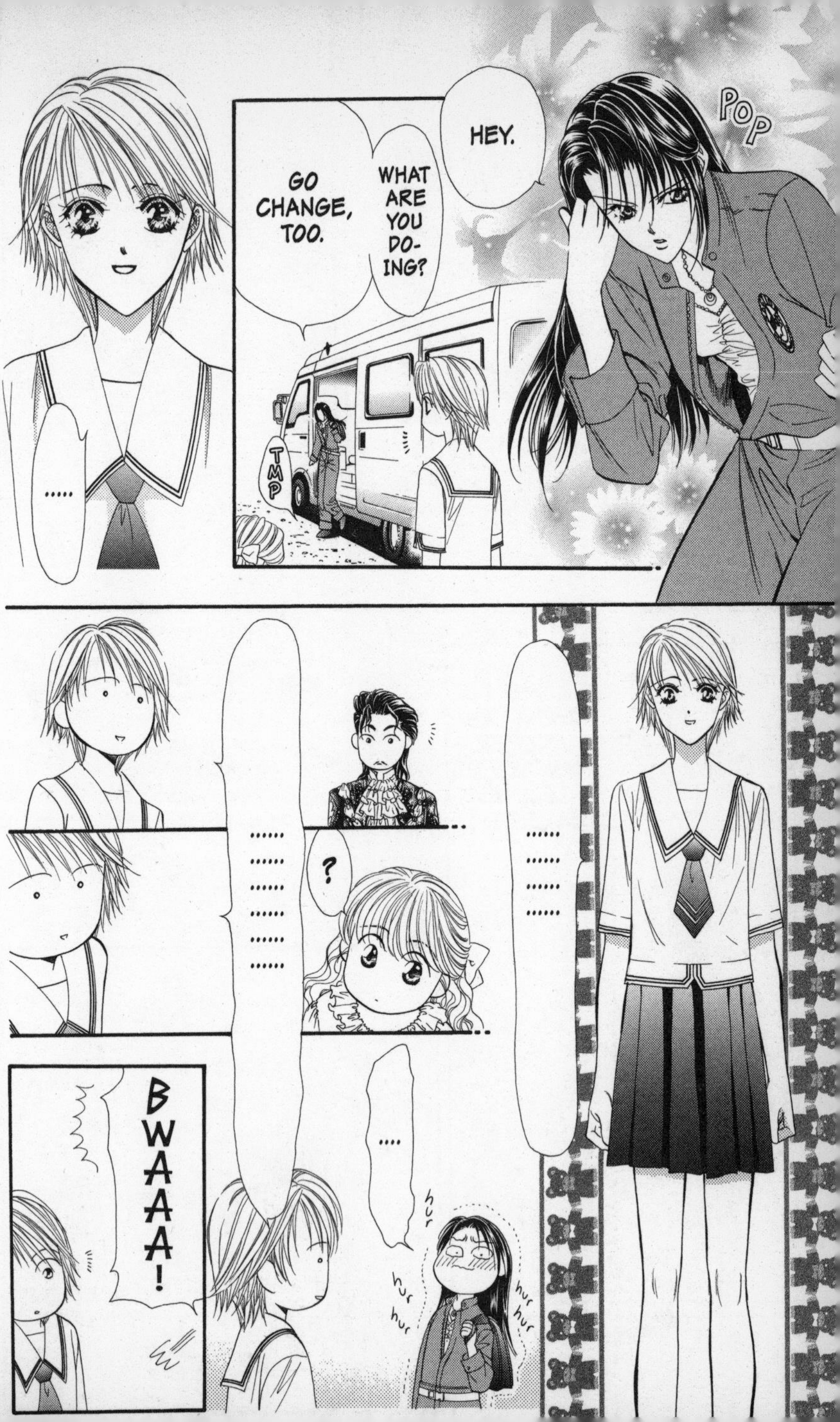
POP
HEY.
WHAT ARE YOU DO-ING?
GO CHANGE, TOO.
TMP
......
......
......
......
......
?
......
......
......
......
......
......
....
hur
hur hur
hur hur
BWAAAA!

WHAT ...?
ha ha ha
YOU WANT TO KEEP WEARING THE UNIFORM THAT MUCH?!
bwa ha ha
!!
N- NO!
THAT'S NOT TRUE!
That has nothing to do with it!
OH, COME ON. WHEN YOU FOUND OUT THAT WE WERE GOING TO WEAR A GIRL'S SCHOOL UNIFORM...
...YOU WERE REALLY REALLY HAPPY.
AND I SAW YOU PLAYING STUDENT AT THE SCHOOL WE USED FOR THE SHOOT.
Good morning, class.
SHOOP
Good morning, teacher.
BLUSH
M...
Moko, you fool! How can you be so shameless?!
KASHOO
SH...
SLAM
SHAMELESS!
BWAHAHA HA
ARE YOU REALLY A TEEN-AGER, TALKING LIKE THAT?!
HA HA HA HA HA
embarrassed
.....

KYOKO... IS ACTING STRANGE.

WHY DOES SHE LIKE UNIFORMS?

I hate having to wear a uniform every morning.

School is boring, too.

I DON'T HAVE TO WEAR A UNIFORM TO SCHOOL.

...

RIGHT?

....

AND...

...

OH, IS THAT SO?

...IT'S NOT THAT SHE LIKES UNIFORMS.
What?
THEN WHAT DOES SHE LIKE?
...
WELL...
...LET ME PUT IT ANOTHER WAY...
MAYBE SHE WANTS AN ORDINARY SCHOOL LIFE WHERE SHE CAN WEAR HER UNIFORM EVERY MORNING AND COMPLAIN ABOUT IT.
OH? THEN HER CURRENT SCHOOL LIFE IS FULL OF UPS AND DOWNS?
....
Whaaat?! She IS weird!
That's my BIG sis! She's different from me!
SHE'S NOT...
...ATTENDING SCHOOL.
WHAT?!
FREEZE
SHE WON'T SAY...
...WHY SHE ISN'T...
K...
Kyoko... your life is full of ups and downs!
She doesn't have a father, and it seems like there are problems with her mother...
THERE MUST BE...

Chak
...SOMETHING SHE CAN'T TALK ABOUT...
......
IT WAS JUST FOR A LITTLE WHILE, BUT...
...I COULD PRETEND TO BE A HIGH SCHOOL STUDENT.
IT WAS FUN...

THANK YOU...
Thank you...
tug tug
She's shaking hands.
I'll never forget about you...
STARTING TODAY...
...I'LL...
...FORGET ABOUT HIGH SCHOOL...
slap slap
All right, switch back into normal mode!
Yeah!
...COMPLETELY!
WAAH
M-MARIA.
WHAT HAPPENED?
KYOKO...
...YOUR PARTY!
HUH?
?
IT'S YOUR PARTY TONIGHT!
LET'S FORGET ABOUT EVERYTHING AND HAVE A MERRY TIME!
WHAT?
NO... BUT...

...I WAS GOING TO SHOW UP FOR WORK TODAY...
...since I'd taken days off for shootings and such...
N-O!
yank yank
tugtug
.....
YOU SHOULD ENJOY LIFE MORE!
Um... well... to enjoy life, I need money...
It's all right. They arranged the party for us. It'd be rude if we didn't attend.
What?! Really?
umm, ahh ...
Then... I guess I'll drop by for a while.
Yes!

I'm not letting you go home tonight!
heh
Whaaat, no, please!
THAT GIRL ...
... SEEMS ...
...TO BE SHOULDERING ...
...A PARENT ...
...CAN HATE HIS OWN CHILD...
DO I...
...STILL NEED...
...HER APPROVAL ?
...A LOT OF HEAVY BURDENS ...

.....

SENIOR
HIGH
SCHOOL
...

AH
...

The next
day.

UHHHHHHG...
His face is all red.
shiver shake
Chill
waddle waddle
Looks fat because of heavy clothing.
Walking weirdly.
MR. YASHIRO...
...CHOO!
YOU'RE IN WORSE SHAPE THAN YOU WERE YESTERDAY.
Obviously.
YOU SHOULD TAKE THE DAY OFF...
NO NO.
There's nothing to worry about.
I'M FINE, JUST FI–
FWONK
Oops.
....
....
?
MR. YASHIRO?
snap
snap
snap

SHA
UH!
BOMPH
Oh no. Hey.
MR. YASHIROOOOOO!
SO.
AS YOU KNOW, PEOPLE KEEP COMING DOWN WITH THIS COLD IN THE OFFICE.
EVERYONE IS BEARING THE BRUNT OF THIS, SO THERE'S NO ONE ELSE WHO'S FREE.
WHAT?
ring ring
Yes, LME Actors Section.
YEAH...I KNOW THAT SHE WANTS TO JOIN A DIFFERENT SECTION...
koff koff
hack hack
shuff shuff
flip flip
H Those who are still healthy. C Those who have a cold.
I ALREADY HAVE MS. KOTONAMI AS A DAIMANE* FOR ANOTHER PERSON.
WHAT?
NO?
* Substitute manager
Matsushima, Supervisor of Actors Section

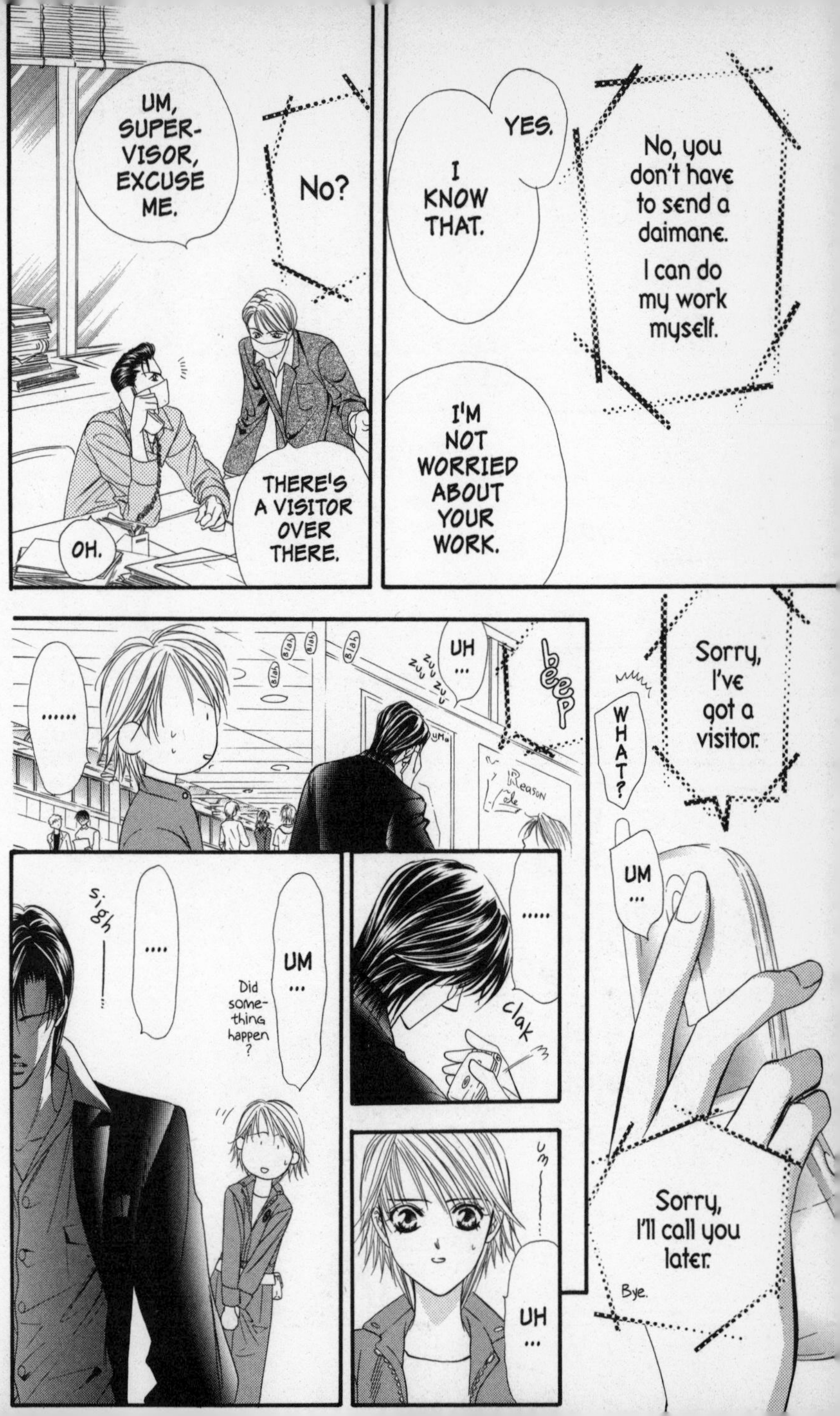
No, you don't have to send a daimane. I can do my work myself.
YES.
I KNOW THAT.
I'M NOT WORRIED ABOUT YOUR WORK.
No?
UM, SUPERVISOR, EXCUSE ME.
OH.
THERE'S A VISITOR OVER THERE.
Sorry, I've got a visitor.
WHAT?
UM ...
Sorry, I'll call you later.
Bye.
beep
UH ...
zuu zuu zuu
Blah
Blah
Blah
......
......
clak
um—
UH ...
UM ...
Did something happen?
....
sigh—

fwish
YOU...
...CAN LEAVE NOW.
clip clop
WHAT?
I'M FINE BY MYSELF.
I CAN'T DO THAT.
What?
SUPERVISOR MATSUSHIMA ASKED ME TO TAKE CARE OF YOU, MR. TSURUGA.
....
clip clop clip clop
I'M SORRY, BUT THERE'S NOTHING THAT NEEDS TO BE TAKEN CARE OF. WHAT'S MORE...
clip clop
...I DON'T THINK THERE'S ANYTHING YOU CAN DO AS MY MANAGER.
annoyed
URK
HOW RUDE... I CAN DO THE JOB OF A MANAGER, TOO.
mumble
In a really small voice.
HALT
?!!!
EEP
HMPH.
REALLY.
SMI-ILE
gentlemanly

WHY?! WHY DO I ALWAYS WILLINGLY STEP ON THE LANDMINE?!
I'LL HAVE YOU TAKE CARE OF ME THEN.
IF YOU INSIST THAT MUCH.
I-
I DIDN'T, I DIDN'T! I JUST WHISPERED LIKE THE BUZZING OF A MOSQUITO!
NUHUH!
panicked
NOOOOOO!
He smiled it! His lying, mean, GENTLEMANLY SMIIIILE!
EEE!!!!
LET'S HAVE YOU WORK SO THAT I'LL BE FORCED TO THANK YOU.
THAT'S IMPOSSIBLE! WHEN YOU'RE SMILING LIKE THAT, THERE'S NO WAY YOU'LL THANK ME HONESTLY!
You'd probably keep harassing me all the time we're together!
THEN...
...I'LL STAMP THE "FULL MARKS" STAMP AS A THANK-YOU.
HE'LL STAMP A "-100 POINTS" FOR SURE!

End of Act 31

Extra Manga

A Scary Story That Really Happened

REN TSURUGA.
DIAMONDS LOOK GREAT ON YOU.
WAIT FOR ME. I'LL GIVE YOU ONE SOON.
MY CHOICEST DIAMOND PIERCED EAR-RING!
ha ha ha
THIS FACE, THIS BODY... THIS IS THE MAN WHO'S FITTING TO BE BY MY SIDE...
Ah...I want to put my Brand on his ear...
poit
MS. ERIKA...
WEREN'T YOU GOING TO JOIN LME TO PREVENT KANAE KOTONAMI FROM BECOMING AN ACTRESS?
MAYBE... HE'S THE REAL REASON YOU WANT TO JOIN?
URK
WH-WHAT ARE YOU SAYING? WHAT ARE YOU SAYING?! OF COURSE! MY OBJECTIVE IS TO INTERFERE WITH THAT IMPUDENT KANAE KOTONAMI'S LIFE!
Of course!
.....
ploop
HUH?
To be continued...

Skip·Beat!

Act 32: Her Lost Youth

Continued
OOOOH!
A PHOTOGRAPH OF REN TSURUGA!
AND IT LOOKS LIKE A PRIVATE PHOTO TAKEN FROM CLOSE-UP!
SNAK
splat
drib
...
?
chiki chiki
gloop
?
chikichiki
CHIKICHIKI
SHAKSHAK
GWAAAA
DRI--BBLE...
KYAAAAAAAAA!!
OH?
I HEARD THERE WAS A VISITOR, SO I RUSHED OVER HERE.
SHE WENT HOME.
whirr whirr whirr
I'LL NEVER LET ANYBODY JOIN LME WHO'S AFTER REN!
As long as I live!
Mail-order cursing toy
End
...so this was one reason why Maria was wandering about in the audition venue...

WHAT?
REN'S DAIMANE?
BECAUSE THERE WAS NO ONE ELSE...
...MATSUSHIMA ASKED MS. MOGAMI.
OH...
Blah Blah
Blah Blah
YES.
STARTING YESTERDAY, APPARENTLY.
Mask to Prevent Colds
HM~~PH...
...
Lory's Assistant
kick
sha
UM...
...PRESIDENT...
...IF YOU NEED TO CONTACT MS. MOGAMI RIGHT AWAY...
...SHE HAS A CELL PHONE...
WHAT?!

What LME Stands For

When *Skip•Beat!* began, there were three people who set up LME, and LME stood for the initials of those three. Well...but I had only decided on "L" for Lory at that time... The name LME came to me first, so even if I hadn't decided on the other two people's names, it was LME. LME came from...there are probably people who have guessed it...LOVE ME...? I'd decided on LME, and was going to think up of the three founders' names. But...I couldn't develop the story to make the other two appear...actually...even if they appeared...

—To Be Continued—

GOOD! GIVE ME HER PHONE NUMBER!
Bravo!
...
HE REALLY IS EASY TO UNDERSTAND...
WHEN HE FOUND OUT THAT THE LOVE ME PAIR WAS GOING TO DEBUT IN THAT COMMERCIAL, HE WAS OBVIOUSLY SULKING.
I wanted their debut to be more gorgeous.
SULK
I was going to produce their debut.
I don't believe that they're ready to be messengers of love yet...
SULK
BUT... FORTUNATELY HE SEEMS TO HAVE GOTTEN OVER IT, AND HE'S IN A GOOD MOOD NOW...
HAS HE GOTTEN OVER IT?
TO ME, HE STILL SEEMS TO BE THINKING THAT "EVEN IF THEY'VE MADE THEIR DEBUT, MY 'LAUNCH OUT INTO THE WORLD! THE MESSENGERS OF LOVE PROJECT'♫ ISN'T DEAD YET."
HMM...
That's true.
EVEN IF THEY'VE MADE THEIR DEBUT, THE PRESIDENT STILL PLAYS AROUND WITH THEM...
...I FEEL SORRY FOR...
...THE LOVE ME MEMBERS.
GLOOM...

TODAY'S...
...MY SECOND DAY AS MR. TSURUGA'S SUBSTITUTE MANAGER.
TO TELL THE TRUTH...
...I DIDN'T GET ANYTHING DONE YESTERDAY.
Next, Show S TV By 2 o'clock.
At 3:30, we come Back.
At 6, we leave and go to the K Studio.
After that, we come Back again and shoot the rest of my cuts.
Eeeee!
DASH DASH
His schedule is packed.
ACTUALLY, IT WAS ALL I COULD DO TO KEEP UP WITH MR. TSURUGA, AND I HAD NO TIME TO BE A MANAGER...
Body and soul.
BUT!
I NOW KNOW HOW BUSY HE IS!
TODAY I WILL DO MY DUTY AS HIS MANAGER!
I made a list of what a manager should do!
To Do

Blah Blah Blah
huh?
BUT...
Thank you for taking the time to see us.
Thank you very much.
Thank you, too.
All right!
HE'S DONE!
ACTUALLY...
HUP
WHA ?!
shup shup
U-UM, PLEASE WAIT! I'LL CARRY YOUR STUFF!
NO.
shup shup
I CAN'T LET A GIRL CARRY MY STUFF.
B-BUT...
...HE CARRIES HIS STUFF.
...THAT'S...
...MY JOB... AS MANAGER.
KYAAAHH!

KYAAAAAAAAAAA!
DASH DASH DASH
He's here! Reeeeen!
!!
EEK
Yoink
?!
KYAAAAAAA
REN!
RE—N!
KYAA!
YAY!! I touched him!!
WATCH OUT.
BUMP
FWUMP
SNAG
huh?!
SO...
KYA
KYA
KYA
...THIS IS MY JOB AS MANA-GER!
I should be protecting you!
HE PROTECTS HER.

MOREOVER...

KABOOM

WAAAAAAAAH! THE SET!

NOOOOOOOOO!

SHE MESSES UP AND MAKES THE ACTOR SHE'S IN CHARGE OF APOLOGIZE.

RAH RAH RAH

I'M SORRY THAT MY MANA-GER...

BOW BOW

I—

I-I'M SORRY, I'M SORRY! SOMEONE SUDDENLY ASKED ME TO CARRY THIS, AND I LOST MY BALANCE!

← People thought she was a grip because of her clothes.

MR. YASHIRO HAS DONE EVERYTHING LIKE ACCEPTING AND SCHEDULING WORK...

...up to a year in advance.

FULL

Yashiro's schedule book

IT'S WORSE THAN YESTER-DAY...

DEPRESSED

IT—

.....

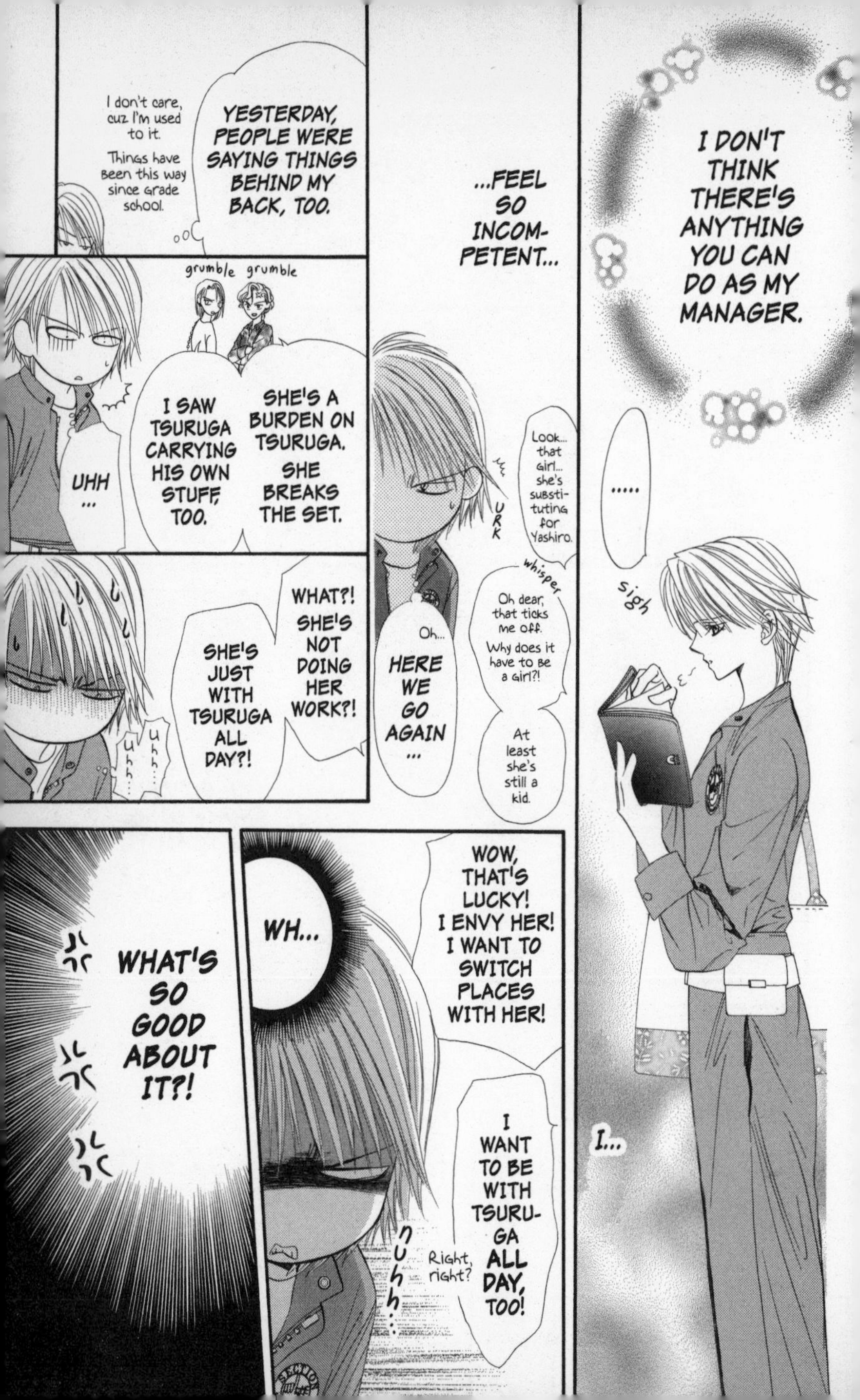
I DON'T THINK THERE'S ANYTHING YOU CAN DO AS MY MANAGER.
.....
sigh
I...
...FEEL SO INCOMPETENT...
URK
Look... that girl... she's substituting for Yashiro.
whisper
Oh dear, that ticks me off. Why does it have to be a girl?!
At least she's still a kid.
Oh... HERE WE GO AGAIN...
YESTERDAY, PEOPLE WERE SAYING THINGS BEHIND MY BACK, TOO.
I don't care, cuz I'm used to it.
Things have been this way since grade school.
grumble grumble
SHE'S A BURDEN ON TSURUGA. SHE BREAKS THE SET.
I SAW TSURUGA CARRYING HIS OWN STUFF, TOO.
UHH...
WHAT?! SHE'S NOT DOING HER WORK?!
SHE'S JUST WITH TSURUGA ALL DAY?!
Uhh... Uhh...
WOW, THAT'S LUCKY! I ENVY HER! I WANT TO SWITCH PLACES WITH HER!
I WANT TO BE WITH TSURUGA ALL DAY, TOO!
Right, right?
nuhh...
WH...
WHAT'S SO GOOD ABOUT IT?!

Going off to the next job.
SILENCE...
In the car, talking is strictly prohibited.
YOU DON'T KNOW HOW UNCOMFORTABLE IT IS WHEN I'M ALONE WITH HIM!
If you want to switch places with me, GO ahead!
I'VE HEARD ABOUT NO SHOES, BUT NO TALKING...?
EXHAUSTED
Oh... I feel like I'm suffocating...
.....
Peek
I...
...FEEL LIKE HE'S BEEN ANGRY SINCE YESTERDAY...
...BECAUSE...
...OF WHAT I SAID?
I CAN DO THE JOB OF A MANAGER, TOO.
AND... THIS IS HOW THINGS TURN OUT.
Of course he'd be angry... I'd be angry, too... and pray for the guy's misfortune.
.....

I- I'M SORRY ...
murmur
......
WHAT?
......
I TOOK THE JOB OF A MANAGER LIGHTLY ...
...AND BECAUSE I SUBSTITUTED AS YOUR MANAGER ...
pi
yellow
...I CAUSED EXTRA TROUBLE FOR YOU, MR. TSURUGA!
Because I'm an idiot, I made you bow in apology.
I'm really really sorry!
bow bow bow bow
......
.... YOU ...
...SAID THE SAME THING JUST A WHILE AGO.
Right after the set was fixed.
I'M NOT SO ANGRY THAT YOU NEED TO APOLOGIZE TO ME TWICE...
WHAT?!
I apologized for nothing?!
NOOOO.
YOU'RE LYING!
THEN WHAT'S THIS TENSE ATMOSPHERE THAT'S BEEN FLOATING AROUND SINCE YESTERDAY?!
I said "It's okay," right?
heh

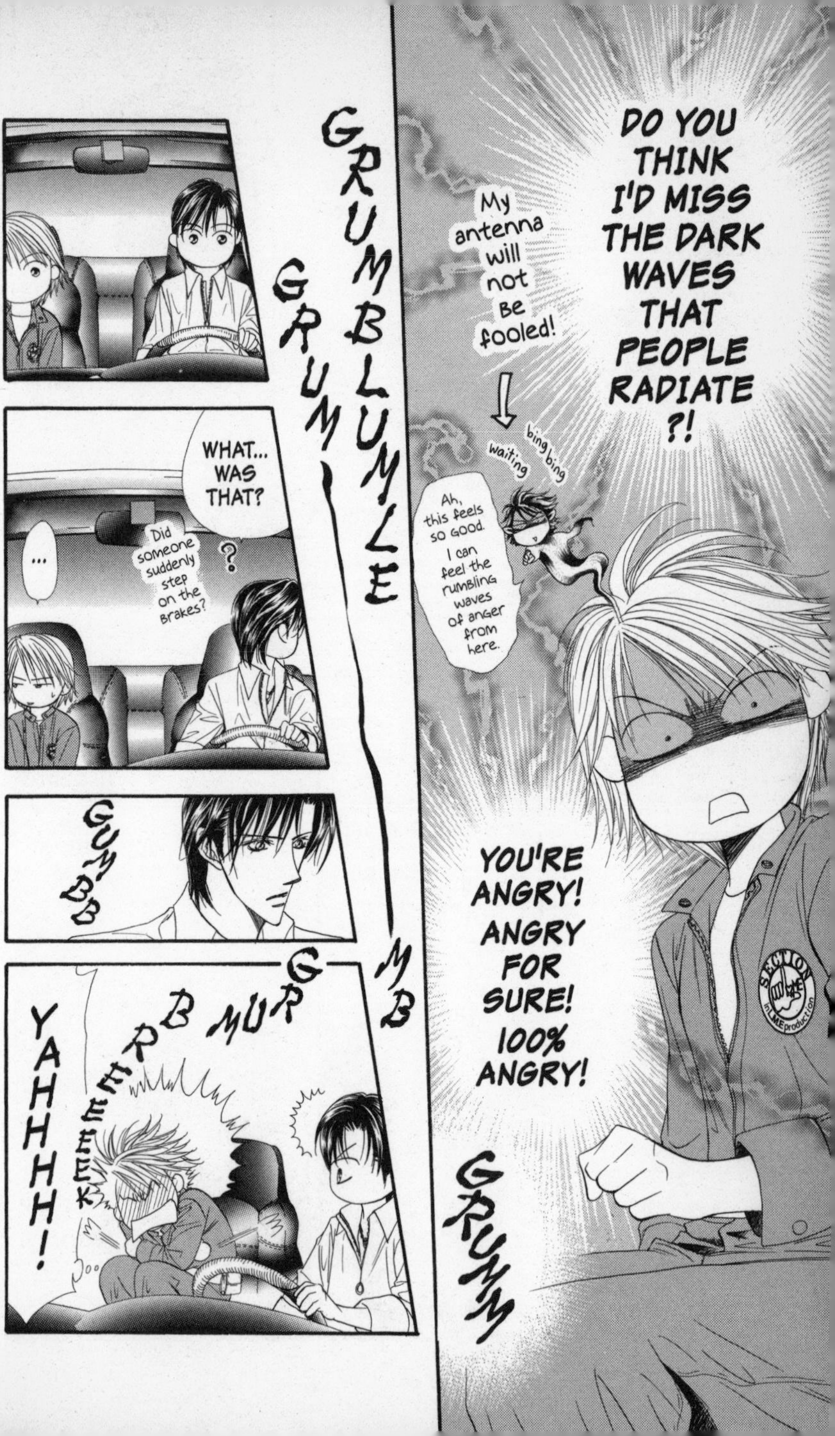DO YOU THINK I'D MISS THE DARK WAVES THAT PEOPLE RADIATE?!
My antenna will not be fooled!
bing bing
waiting
Ah, this feels so good. I can feel the rumbling waves of anger from here.
YOU'RE ANGRY! ANGRY FOR SURE! 100% ANGRY!
GRUMM
GRUMBLUMBLE
GRUM
WHAT... WAS THAT?
Did someone suddenly step on the brakes?
?
...
GUMBB
MB
GRUMB
RRB
YAHHHHH!
EEEEK

I Was Surprised, Too

When I think about it, the first time the script "The Forest of Spirals" appeared was in the chapter when Ren was having problems with "tentekomai"...To tell the truth, I created that script on the spot just for the line using "tentekomai." So I had only a vague image of the contents and Ren's role, and I thought that the script would never appear..

> Forest of Spirals

...But it appeared... 🎵 Again... 🎵🎵 I don't watch many dramas, but I thought about whether it was possible to appear in another drama at the same time (there were actors who were... 🎵) and there were other things I was pondering about... 🎵🎵 I wondered how true it was to the way dramas are shot nowadays...But I used "The Forest of..." anyway.

—To Be Continued—

...MAYBE YOU'RE HUNGRY?

OH...

WHAT?

Wha... no...

Why?

7:30

Huh?!

H-Her stomach is making a skidding noise!

Ah!

OH! IT'S ALREADY SO LATE!

I wasn't thinking!

A-a box dinner?

WHAT?!

...DID YOU GET ONE?

THERE WERE BOX DINNERS AT THE LAST PLACE...

Oh.

I'M SORRY, OF COURSE YOU'RE HUNGRY.

THERE ARE SOME PLACES THAT DON'T HAVE THEM.

Ahh.

Useless once again.

AWW...

I-Is he angry?

The crew told me, but...they didn't tell her...

Proof that they don't trust her as manager.

I didn't think there would be one for someone who wasn't going to stay on until the end...

I- I'm sorry.

THEN... LET'S STOP SOMEPLACE AND GET SOMETHING TO EAT.
WHAT DO YOU WANT?
Wh...
...HUH?!
Vrooooom
NO...
B-BUT...
um
WE DON'T HAVE TIME FOR...
IT'S ALL RIGHT.
WE'RE ON SCHEDULE.
Actually, they lost some time due to Kyoko's blunders, but Ren acted with almost no retakes.
WE DROVE HERE PRETTY QUICKLY...
...SO WE HAVE ENOUGH TIME TO EAT.
smile
....
OH...
I'M NOT SO ANGRY THAT YOU NEED TO APOLOGIZE TO ME TWICE...
IT...
IT SEEMS TO BE TRUE...
It's not his lying gentle-manly smile...
nervous
I-I WONDER WHY...
I...
...FEEL THERE'S NO REASON TO STAY ANGRY...
...WHEN SOME-ONE'S ADMITTED TO BEING WRONG ONCE...
AH...

THEN...
SO?
WHAT DO YOU WANT TO EAT?
...IF HE'S NOT ANGRY AT MY BLUNDERS AS HIS MANA-GER...
...I WONDER WHAT HE IS ANGRY ABOUT...
UH...
...UH... MM...
WHAT-EVER YOU WANT TO EAT, MR. TSURU-GA.
...THAT'S...
...THE WAY HE IS...
...YES...
...I GET IT...

Vroo
oom
.....
....
....
Maybe... he doesn't have anything particular in mind?
ALL RIGHT ...
... WHAT ABOUT THIS?
GRILLED WHOLE FROGS.
IT'S A POPULAR GROSS FOOD.
SIZZZ...
NOOOOOO!
tic
OH.
IT'S EIGHT.
TSURUGA MUST BE GOING OFF TO HIS NEXT JOB.
I HOPE HE'S EATING PROP-ERLY.
HE SHOULD BE.
cough cough
PONK PONK PONK
THAT'S WHY I ASSIGNED HER TO BE WITH REN.
sff sff

SO... YOU SENT HER WITH HIM JUST SO THAT HE EATS PROPERLY ?!
That would make every woman in Japan envious and jealous!
Even I envy her!
EX-ACTLY.
matter-of-fact
Here.
I'm not expecting her to do the work of a manager at all.
ACCORD-ING TO YASHIRO, IF YOU LEAVE REN ALONE...
...BECAUSE HE'S BUSY AND FINDS IT BOTHERSOME, AND HIS HUNGER IMPULSE IS NUMB...
No appe-tite.
...HE COULD GO FOR DAYS WITHOUT EATING ANYTHING.
Hmmm...a dieter would kill for a body like that!
When he's got to take care of his body for his job!
YASHIRO'S NEVER SEEN HIM EAT ALL OF HIS BOX LUNCHES ...
...and...
...WHEN HE EATS ON HIS OWN, HE DRINKS THOSE JELLY POWER DRINKS.
PONK PONK PONK
WOW... I HAD NO IDEA...
HE'S SO DEDICATED TO HIS WORK, THOUGH ...
It's even worse than what I'd heard...
It's totally unexpected...
I KNOW THAT HE WON'T BE ABLE TO LET A GIRL EAT BY HERSELF.
SO ...
...NOT CARING FOR HIS BODY IS HIS WEAK POINT ...
tap tap
...BUT BEING CONSID-ERATE IS HIS STRONG POINT.
IF SHE'S WITH HIM, HE'LL EAT FOR SURE.

Sizzz~~~zz
SOME-THING, AT LEAST.
Sparrrkle~
OH, HOW MANY MONTHS HAS IT BEEN?!
Since I ran away from Kyoto?!
This aroma that tickles my sense of smell!
The sound that sinks into my sense of hearing!
Sizzz~
JOY
You're not the leading actor, but by just lying there, you fulfill my sense of sight and my heart.
You, the round and smooth and yellow you!
THEN THIS IS YOUR LAST CHANCE.
Or we go for the frog.
WHAT DO YOU WANT TO EAT?
HUH...

HAM-BURGER STEAK!
WITH A FRIED EGG ON IT!
Grip
Grip
....
She loves ham-burger steaks.
snarf snarf
chomp chomp
YES... I REMEMBER...
CORN!
CORN, LOOK! THIS STONE LOOKS LIKE A HAMBURGER!
It's round and flat.
OH, BUT THIS IS A HAMBURGER, TOO!
Oh, this one, too!
This is great! Let's make this place a Hamburger Kingdom!
...
THEN WHAT ABOUT THIS?
YOUR MAJESTY, KING HAMBURGER!
Curtsey
You're in excellent health!
....
EXTRA LARGE
tp
shaking in amusement
heh heh heh heh
shaking in amusement
....

M-MR. TSURUGA... WHAT HAPPENED?
Blah Blah Blah Blah
WHAT?
OH.
Noth-ing.
YOU EAT AS IF THE FOOD'S... REALLY DELICIOUS.
heh heh
....
IS HE MAK-ING FUN OF ME?
IT IS DELI-CIOUS.
MUST BE...
tender
th-thump
WH-
clak clak
munch munch
WHAT WAS THAT?!
HEY, CUZ, HE REALLY LOOKS LIKE HIM.

WHAAAT?!
yammer yammer
BUT THIS IS A FAMILY RESTAU-RANT.
HE CAN'T BE HERE.
BUT ...
AND LOOK AT WHAT HE'S EATING!
IT'S A HAM-BURGER STEAK! THERE'S NO WAY IT'S REN!
Ren wouldn't eat such things!
MR. TSURUGA... THAT'S WHY I SAID YOU SHOULD ORDER SOME-THING ELSE...
ONCE YOU EAT IT, IT'S ALL THE SAME.
He doesn't want to bother think-ing about what to eat.
AND LOOK AT THE GIRL HE'S WITH!
IT'S SOME SORT OF WORK UNIFORM!
AND IT'S WEIRD!
It's too tacky!
I can't have Ren walking with a girl like that!
YES, YES, IT MUST BE WEIRD.
HEH
NO, BUT SHE LOOKS LIKE SHE'S OUR AGE, SO SHE MIGHT BE IN HIGH SCHOOL...
URK
...AND MAYBE THAT'S HER WAY OF "DRESSING UP" AFTER SCHOOL.
Whaaat?!

IF YOU'RE GONNA WEAR SOMETHING LIKE THAT, WEAR YOUR UNIFORM!
At least that would look much better.
Yeah.
THERE'RE LOTS OF GUYS WHO'LL GIVE YOU MONEY IF YOU WEAR YOUR UNIFORM.
Yeah yeah.
WE CAN ONLY USE THE "SCHOOL GIRL" BRAND NOW.
She's stupid.
SHE'S LETTING HER YOUTH ROT AWAY.
SO I COULDN'T BECOME A HIGH SCHOOL GIRL!
It's not my fault!
KYA HA HA HA HA
YOU'RE A FAILURE AS A HIGH SCHOOL GIRL!
GRRRRR
Bend
YOU THREE GIRLS ARE THE STUPID ONES!
THE "SCHOOL GIRL" BRAND ?!
evil aura
crack
SHATTER
I'M A FAILURE AS A HIGH SCHOOL GIRL?!
AHHH!
CLATTER
cra-sh
shatter
HYUUUUUU
CRUNCH
AHHH! WHAT? WHAT?! WHAT'S GOING ON?! WHAT'S WRONG WITH THIS PLACE ?!
There's some-thing here!
hee hee hee
heh heh heh

Aaaaaugh, sheesh!
IF I HADN'T BEEN DUPED BY A DORK LIKE THAT...
...AND GIVEN MY LIFE FOR HIM...
...I WOULD BE ENJOYING MY SECOND YEAR OF HIGH SCHOOL!
KSSS! SHOTAROO!!
WHEN I THINK THAT YOU'RE IN YOUR SECOND YEAR OF HIGH SCHOOL, I GO CRAZY WITH A GRUDGE!
EVIL AURA
fwuuu
...was totally dark...
A Kaleidoscope of her pitch-black life.
Her dark life was from age 6 to 13.
...myyyy liiiife...
14...
15...
16...
slither
slither
slither
honk honk
huh?
I DID IT AGAIN!
vroooom
I ALWAYS LOSE MYSELF WHEN I THINK ABOUT SHOTARO!
OH.
He's waiting for her to come out.
D-DARN!

vroooo——————om
...
H...
HE'S ANGRY!
Of course he'd be!
NO... BUT... I APOLOGIZED...
WHY?
HE'S NOT ANGRY THAT I MADE HIM WAIT?
HIGH SCHOOL ...
WHAT?
... I'VE ...
... NEVER ASKED YOU THIS...
... BUT...

...YOU'RE NOT ATTENDING SCHOOL, RIGHT?

BLUNT

UHH...

He mentions exactly what I don't want him to talk about right now!

IS THE REASON FOR THAT...

...SHO FUWA?

FOR HIM...
...I WAS ONLY A STEPPING STONE...
...TO JOIN SHOWBIZ.
ONCE HE WAS IN SHOW-BIZ...
...HE DIDN'T NEED ME ANY-MORE...
HEY, HEY.
SHO...
...IS MY PRINCE.
Hamburger steak stones
WHEN I GROW UP...
...HE'LL COME AND GET ME, HOLDING GLASS SLIPPERS.

SO I'LL BECOME A PRINCESS...
...AND MARRY SHO IN THE FUTURE!
.....
I REMEMBER...
...HER SPEAKING FONDLY OF HIM.
THAT "SHO" WAS FUWA.
...
Now he realizes.
I'M...
...GOING TO BECOME A BIGGER STAR THAN HE IS...
...AND HAVE MY REVENGE!
HE DARED TO CALL ME A HOUSEKEEPER. I'LL FORCE HIM TO SAY "I SHOULDN'T HAVE DITCHED YOU"!
THAT'S WHY...
...YOU'RE STUDYING ACTING.

...SEEM TO HAVE YOUR OWN REASONS...

YOU...

WHAT?

...BUT IF THAT'S WHY YOU WANT TO BECOME AN ACTRESS...

tense

...AS AN ACTOR...

...I FIND IT UNPLEAS-ANT.

AH!
This tense atmosphere!
nyooo
tense
Ah, this feels so good. I can feel the rumbling waves of anger from here.
TH...
MR. TSURUGA...
Antenna
...HEARD FROM SOMEWHERE THAT I'M STUDYING ACTING...
...AND HE THOUGHT I WAS DOING IT TO HAVE MY REVENGE AGAINST SHOTARO...
THIS IS IT!
...AND HE WAS SILENTLY ANGRY SINCE YESTERDAY!
N...
NO! MR. TSURUGA!
Hey.
SHA
No.
I'M STUDYING ACTING BECAUSE...
KLONK
DID YOU FORGET WE'RE IN A CAR?
It was... too late.

BRR
BRR BRR BRR BRR BRR
eh?
shup
BRR BRR BRR
...
dig dig
BRR BRR BRR
OH.
pi Green
THE CELL PHONE...
BRR BRR
THEY GAVE ME THIS...
I forgot about it...
MS. MO-GAMI...
...YOU FOOOOOOL!
I've been calling you over and over since this morning!
Why didn't you answer?!
UPSET
IT'S THE PRESI-DENT...
I'M SORRY! I DON'T HAVE A CELL PHONE...
I...
...SO I PUT IT ON SILENT MODE, AND DIDN'T NOTICE THAT YOU'D CALLED...

Pout
....
I was going to give you some good news, but now I don't feel like it.
vuu~~
HUH ...
WH-WHAT IS IT?
What's the good news?!
Um...
Y-YES...
Maybe I don't really want to hear it...
This...doesn't sound good...
Uh oh...
EEP
You wanna hear it?
bwee hee hee
....
You don't seem to want to hear it.
The way you answered me.
WHAAT? R-REALLY?
eh heh heh heh heh
...
This is getting boring.
kachak
kachak
Maybe I should just cancel...
...your enrollment in high school.

I know a gooooood school that you can transfer to. They allow students to work in showbiz while attending school.
WHAT?!
I guess...
...you don't want to go, Ms. Mogami.
Y...
YES, I DOOOOOOO!

End of Act 32

AN ACQUAINTANCE OF MINE IS THE PRINCIPAL OF A HIGH SCHOOL.
THEY HAVE A PERFORMING ARTS CLASS, AND THEY ARE PRETTY FLEXIBLE.
I CAN GO TO HIGH SCHOOL!
Don't worry, the transfer exam is an easy test of general knowledge and a review of middle school.
I CAN GO TO HIGH SCHOOL!
Just reviewing a little should be enough.
I'D PRETTY MUCH GIVEN UP ON IT.
What about it, Ms. Mogami?

I want to talk over the details with you.
Do you want to go?
I CAN...
Y...
YES!
PLEASE!
...GO TO HIGH SCHOOL TOO!
I'LL COME RIGHT OVER!

Skip·Beat!

Act 33: An Emergency Situation

OH.
THEN YOU DIDN'T DROP BY MR. YASHIRO'S PLACE BEFORE COMING HERE THIS MORNING.
THAT'S RIGHT.
HE SCOLDED ME YESTERDAY, SAYING THAT I SHOULDN'T COME.
HE SAID HE'D HAVE SOMEONE FROM HOME COME OVER.
He's terrible, isn't he?
I was so worried.
I thought he might be dead because he lives alone.
hee hee
HE DOESN'T WANT YOU TO CATCH HIS COLD.
fluff fluff
THERE'S NOTHING TO WORRY ABOUT.
I CAN BOAST THAT I'VE NEVER EVER CAUGHT A COLD.
WHAT?
REAAAALLY?

What LME Stands For (continued)

...I think that the characters of the other two might have become like Lory, obsessed with love, so they would have been very annoying. Or since Lory is like THAT, if I made the other two ordinary people, they'd have been overshadowed by Lory and become characters that weren't really needed...in reality, M&E didn't have a chance to appear and weren't born, but now I think about it, I believe it was a good idea not to have them appear ...and because the other two didn't appear, M&E became meaningless, and I was in a bind...So I consulted my editor and thought up something for M&E. That's the THING that appears when Lory appears.

—Continued—

SNAP
.....
.....
shake shake shake shake
GRR GRR GRR GRR
TH...
The lead broke.
...I'VE SEEN IT BEFORE.
THIS PROBLEM...
THIS QUESTION!
THE ARRANGEMENT OF NUMBERS!
HOW COULD I FORGET?!
THAT TIME! I WAS DUPED BY YOUR IMPERTINANCE, AND I...
YES!
..I!

...GOT ANOTHER DEEP WOUND IN MY HEART!
A ONE-IN-A-MILLION-CHANCE FOR REVENGE! I'LL HAVE MY REVENGE NOW!
NYOOO
click click click click
SKRI TCH SKRITCH SKRITCH
FLIP FLIP FLIP
heh heh heh keh
keh heh heh heh
...
...
I'll do this, do this, do this to you!
T-TSURUGA... WHAT'S HAP-PENED... TO HER?
Sh-She's a bit... scary... Her aura...
OH...
...SHE...
...HAS AN EXAM SOON...
WELL... YES...
AN EXAM?
AT SCHOOL?
I'D... ASSUMED THAT SHE WASN'T ATTENDING SCHOOL...
Because she's a daimane...
SHE'S RADIATING THIS SPINE-CHILLING AURA...

...But...even if nothing concrete was decided in the Beginning, I didn't think "The Forest of..." would turn into a detective drama... When Ren was struggling with "tentekomai" he was dressed up as...a gigolo?)"... At that time, according to me, "The Forest of..." was a slightly mysterious drama with the night Business as the setting...

The Messiah for Colds

My mother often makes this for me when I have a cold and a sore throat. (But the daikon is cut into cubes.) When I eat this (which has Been chilled in the fridge) when I've got a high fever, I feel refreshed. The daikon juice is just sweet enough with the honey, and soothes my sore throat...that's what I feel...yes. Anyway, even if I don't have an appetite, I can eat this...I can...I'll say it many times, Because I think there are readers who think, "That must taste Bad". It doesn't taste Bad... I don't think so.

ARE HER GRADES SO BAD THAT SHE NEEDS TO STUDY THAT DESPERATELY?
That girl...
You! You! You! You!
SCRITCH SCRITCH
....
no Mogami
88
th-thump

hic
I COULDN'T GET A 100% ON THE CRAM SCHOOL TEST...
sob
sob
I'LL...
...BE SCOLDED BY MOTHER AGAIN...
I...
...WONDER...
...WHY I'M SO STUPID...
SN
AP

....
NOW THAT I THINK ABOUT IT...
I REALIZE NOW...
...SOMEBODY WHO NEVER SCORED BELOW AN 80% USUALLY WOULDN'T BE CALLED STUPID...
She IS stupid.
heh
WELL...
...OF COURSE I WAS BRAINWASHED...
BE-CAUSE ...
...I WAS ALWAYS MERCILESSLY TOLD...
...that I was stupid.
THERE WERE NO "GOOD GRADES" OR "BAD GRADES" IN MY LIFE.
I WAS PRAISED ONLY IF I GOT A "100%."

IF I COULDN'T FULFILL HER EXPECTATIONS...
...THAT MEANT...
...THAT I...
...WAS A FAILURE...
CUT!
YES, LET'S DO THIS SCENE THAT WAY.
...huh?
Take!
Yes!
Oh, it's starting.
HUH?

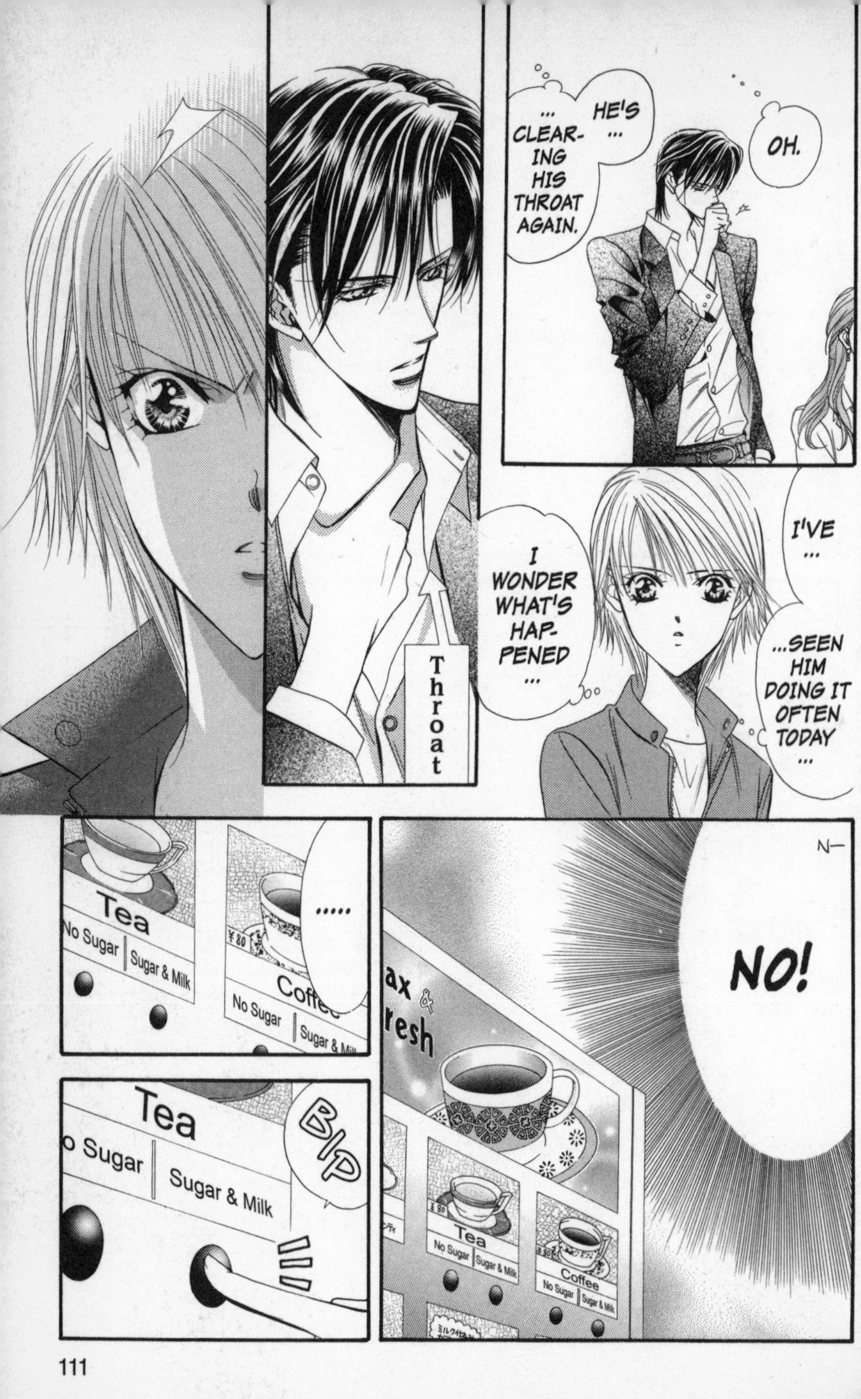
OH.
HE'S ... ... CLEARING HIS THROAT AGAIN.
Throat
I'VE ...
...SEEN HIM DOING IT OFTEN TODAY ...
I WONDER WHAT'S HAPPENED ...
N—
NO!
Tea
No Sugar
Sugar & Milk
Coffee
.....
B/P

SHOOM
CHING
IT'S AN EXTRA-ORDINARY SITUATION.
....
STARE
Peek
Y-You surprised me.
WHAT'RE YOU DOING?
Over there.
MR. TSU-RU-GA...
I saw it.
With my own eyes.
YOU... GOT TEA WITH SUGAR AND MILK.
WHY?
HUH?
Well...
I JUST FELT LIKE IT.
Blah
Blah
Blah
YOU'RE LYING.
BLUNT
...

I'VE ASKED AROUND, AND I KNOW!
YOU ALWAYS HAVE YOUR COFFEE AND TEA STRAIGHT!
And you have your drinks on the rocks!
SMACK
ARE YOU A SPY, OR SOMEONE FROM A DETECTIVE AGENCY?
After she became his daimane, she asked around.
You could've just asked me...
....
BUT...
... YEAH...
...I SEEM TO BE A BIT TIRED...
...SO IT'S TRUE I FELT LIKE DRINKING THIS.
HMPH.
SO WHEN YOU GET TIRED, YOUR THROAT GETS TIRED TOO, MR. TSURUGA?
HMM?
NO? THIS IS THE FIRST TIME THAT'S HAPPENED.
I WONDER HOW SHE KNEW...
...That there's something wrong with my throat.

YOU FEEL LIKE THERE'S SOMETHING STUCK IN YOUR THROAT.
WHEN YOU SWALLOW YOUR SALIVA, THE BACK OF YOUR THROAT FEELS ITCHY.
....
HOW'D YOU KNOW?
IT FEELS EXACTLY LIKE THAT.
....
MR. TSURUGA... DO YOU KNOW WHAT THOSE SYMPTOMS ARE CALLED?
WHAT?
A COLD.
...HEH...
URK☆

MR. TSURUGA, IT'S NOTHING TO LAUGH ABOUT.
THOSE ARE THE INITIAL SYMPTOMS OF A COLD.
TAKE SOME MEDICINE BEFORE IT GETS WORSE.
thonk
NO WAY...
...I'D CATCH A COLD.
I CAN BOAST THAT I'VE NEVER EVER CAUGHT A COLD.
DON'T HANG ONTO YOUR PAST GLORY!
HOW CAN YOU SAY THAT'S NOT A COLD?!
IF YOU HAVEN'T EVER CAUGHT A COLD, MR. TSURUGA, THEN YOU WON'T KNOW WHAT IT'S LIKE!
UH...
Sound argument
I've had colds before, I know what it's like!
It's a cold!
NO, IT'S NOT.
It is!
N-O.
WHY DO YOU KEEP DENYING YOU'VE GOT A COLD?!
WHY DO YOU KEEP TRYING TO CONVINCE ME I'VE GOT A COLD?!
He secretly prided himself on it.

I'M NOT TRYING TO CONVINCE YOU.
YOU'VE GOT A COLD!
YOU MUST'VE CAUGHT IT FROM MR. YASHIRO!
THEN IT'S EVEN MORE UNLIKELY.
I'M NOT SNEEZING, AND I DON'T HAVE A FEVER LIKE MR. YASHIRO!
H-HE'S SERIOUSLY QUIBBLING!
And when he's the polite Ren Tsuruga...
Slack-Jawed Surprise
.....
WELL... ALL RIGHT... LET'S PUT IT THIS WAY.
scrtch scrtch
It is true that this is a bit unusual...
ARE YOU A CHILD ?!
....
LET'S SEE HOW THINGS TURN OUT. IF I START SNEEZING OR GET A FEVER LIKE MR. YASHIRO...
...THEN I'VE GOT A COLD LIKE YOU SAY.
WHA ?!

Y-YOU'RE NOT GOING TO TREAT IT?!
IT'D BE TOO LATE IF YOU GET A FEVER!
clomp clomp
tmp tmp tmp
I'M ALL RIGHT. I TRAIN MY BODY.
I'm not that soft.
WHAT'RE YOU GOING TO DO IF YOU CAN'T SHOW UP FOR WORK?
clomp clomp
tmp tmp tmp
THAT WON'T HAP-PEN.
I'm tough.
YOU MIGHT END UP CRYING LATER.
clomp clomp
tmp tmp tmp
I WON'T CRY.
I'm strong.
You'll regret it!
I won't.
I'm sturdy.
THUS...
...THE SILLY CYCLE OF PER-SUASION AND DENIAL APPAR-ENTLY WENT ON.
chirp chirp chirp chirp
THE NEXT MORNING.

THE MAN...
UU
UU
UU
UU
......
...AND THE WO-MAN.
......
Thermometer
SEEEEEE. I KNEW IT.
GLOOM
UUUUUUUU
His eyes are watery because of the fever.
......
101 F

I- I'M IN SHOCK...
WHY DID I HAVE TO CATCH A COLD...?
WHAT DID I DO WRONG?
DEPRESSED
MR. TSURU-GA...
He's still saying it...
...YOU...
THEY NEVER EXPECTED ME TO DO THE JOB OF A MANAGER!
IT DIDN'T HAVE TO BE ME!
MR. TSURU-GA...
...TO BE BLUNT, YOU'RE...
...A FAILURE AS A PRO.
STAB!
...DON'T USUALLY EAT WELL AT ALL.
URK
!!
chung
sha
WHEN I REPORTED YOUR CONDITION LAST NIGHT, SUPER-VISOR MATSUSHIMA BLURTED THAT OUT.
AND...
...THAT'S THE REASON WHY I WAS ASKED TO BE MR. TSURUGA'S DAIMANE!
Well, I figured that if you were with him, he'd eat properly. And since you're a girl, he'd be even more considerate...
I mean, he IS a gentle-man, so...
THAT WAS QUITE A SHOCK.

I-I CAN'T BELIEVE YOU'RE SAYING THAT!
UAAAAH!
I'M FINISHED!
The polar region of despair
GLOOM
.....
DI-RECTOR KURO-SAKI WAS SAYING ...
...THAT SOME-ONE...
...WHO CAN'T MANAGE HIS BODY, THE TOOL FOR THIS BUSI-NESS...
...LACKS PROFES-SIONAL-ISM.
I DON'T KNOW HOW MUCH YOU TRAIN YOUR BODY...
...BUT YOU CAN'T BE HEALTHY BY JUST TRAINING THE OUTSIDE.
Yack Yack
I CAN UNDERSTAND YOU'RE PRESSED FOR TIME, BUT BUSY PEOPLE MUST EAT WELL!
Otherwise your immunity decreases.
MR. TSURUGA, YOU HAVEN'T EVEN TAKEN YOUR MEDICINE YET!
This is the crew parking lot at the shot location.

SORRY...
WHAT?
HUH?
IT'S...
...EXACTLY AS YOU SAY.
I WAS...
...TOO CONFIDENT IN MYSELF...
ha ha
THIS IS...
...EMBARRASSING.
IF THIS WAS GOING TO HAPPEN...

...I SHOULD HAVE...
...LISTENED TO YOU...
THAT'S WHY...

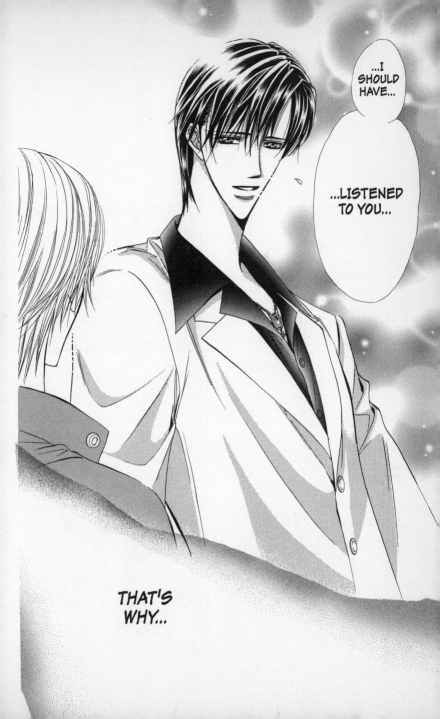

......
...EVERY TIME...
...EVEN IF I DON'T WANT TO...
...I JUST CAN'T HELP THINKING...
...WHEN HE SAYS...
...SOMETHING LIKE THIS NATURALLY...

...THAT HE IS REALLY MATURE ...
ALTHOUGH HE QUIBBLES LIKE A CHILD!
HOW CAN HE SAY "SORRY" SO HONESTLY?!
When he was pompously lectured by a young girl!
I wouldn't, definitely not! I'd keep silent!
Blah
Blah
Blah
Blah
Blah
Math
MORE-OVER ...
...MR. TSURUGA PROBABLY DIDN'T WANT TO HEAR A LECTURE FROM ME MOST OF ALL...
MR. TSU-RU-GA...
...STILL MISUNDER-STANDS...
I-I CAN'T BELIEVE YOU'RE SAYING THAT!
region of despair
AAAAH!
GLOOM
...HE...
...BUT IF THAT'S WHY YOU WANT TO BECOME AN ACT-RESS...
...THAT...

...I'M STUDYING ACTING TO HAVE MY REVENGE AGAINST SHOTARO...
...AS AN ACTOR ...
tense
...I FIND IT UNPLEASANT.
WAIT A MINUTE ...
Blah Blah
Blah
Blah
Hurry up!
...MR. TSURUGA'S CRACKLING AURA...
We'll finish the shooting on schedule!
... I'VE ...
...FELT IT BEFORE, A LONG TIME AGO...
IT...
... WAS ...

DON'T BELIEVE ...
...THAT GUTS ARE EVERYTHING...
...WHEN WE MET...
...FOR THE SECOND TIME!
......

MR. TSURU-GA...
...WAS ANGRY THAT I'D JOINED SHOW-BIZ...
...SIMPLY TO HAVE MY REVENGE AGAINST SHOTARO!
THAT'S WHY MR. TSURUGA WAS MEAN TO ME FROM THE BEGINNING!
WELL, IT DIDN'T RAIN TODAY...
...BUT WE'RE LUCKY IT'S CLOUDY.
Yeah.
REALLY.
THEN WE CAN FUDGE IT USING ARTI-FICIAL RAIN.
clank clank
RAIN WHEN IT'S SUNNY WOULD LOOK FAKE.
We might even get a rainbow.

A-ARTI-FICIAL RAIN?
...uh...
...rain?
clank clank
WERE THEY ABLE TO RENT REHEARSAL ROOMS FOR REN AND YUMIKO, WHO'LL GET SOAKED?
The site manager said no, right?
THEY DID MANAGE TO GET THEM.
At the last minute.
OF COURSE THEY'D DO ANY-THING TO RENT THEM.
WE CAN'T HAVE THOSE TWO CATCH COLDS.
H...
HE HAS A COOOOOLD!
Already!
MR. TSU-RU-Gaaa!
WARRGH!
Stop that shooting!
HUH?
NO WAY!
A SCENE WHERE YOU'LL GET WET!
YOU'VE GOT A FEVER. WHAT'RE YOU GOING TO DO IF IT GETS WORSE?
HMM...
...I CAN'T HELP IT.
I ASKED FOR IT.
I don't deserve any sympathy.
BUT!
AND...

...WE CAN ONLY USE THIS LOCATION TODAY...
zssh
The rain is too strong. Turn it down!
And row A, bring it down a little more.
SO...
...WE HAVE TO SHOOT THIS SCENE NOW.
EVEN...
...IF MY FEVER GETS WORSE...
...OR IF I COLLAPSE...
...I'LL KEEP ACTING...
All right!
Then take.
Take!
zssh
...UNTIL WE CAN SHOOT THE BEST SCENE...

SCENE 31.
READY.
...UNTIL...
BEGIN!
... THE MOMENT ...
...I LOSE CON- SCIOUS- NESS...

End of Act 33

Skip·Beat!

Act 34: Image Crash

zsssh———...
YES, I THINK I WAS AT FAULT...
...BUT I JUST DON'T UNDERSTAND!
BE-CAUSE...
...THERE'S SOMETHING WRONG WITH THAT PERSON.
IT'S EX-TREMELY SPACICI-CIOUS!
WHON———K
OH.
Crew
Crew
Crew

This is LME's Formal Name

This...!!

LORY'S MAJESTIC ENTERTAINMENT

Lory's Majestic Entertain-ment.

Please remember it, everybody.

I SAID IT AGAIN!
Noooo!
I'M SOOORRY!
.....
YUMIKO! IT'S "SUSPICIOUS" NOT "SPACICIOUS"!
Please!
Director
...
I-I'm soooorry.
Waah!
HEY! WILL YOU CUT IT OUT?!
Take 4
IT'S EX-TREMELY ...
SPACI-CICOUS ...
Oops ...
Again!
AND SHE HAS TO DO THIS IN THE RAINY SCENE, OVER AND OVER!
twitch twitch twitch
THIS IS THE THIRD TIME...
WHY CAN'T THAT WOMAN SAY "SUSPICIOUS" ONCE!
twitch twitch
Is she messing around ?!
fume
IS SHE TRYING TO PRETEND TO BE "CUTE" BY GOOFING A LITTLE?!
fume fume twitch fume fume
I'm sorry, Tsuru-Gaaaa.
Take 5
...THAT PERSON. IT'S...
...EX-TREMELY ...
...
Um... um...
She doesn't know which is correct now.
....
Cut!
GRR!

MR. TSURUGA HAS A FEVER!
Yumiko, if it's a retake the next time too, I'll throw this at you!
PONK PONK
Her angry spirit
zssh
...
MR. TSURUGA...
sigh
oh!
...YOU'RE LOOKING PALE...
shrink
....
EVEN IF THEY CAN'T CANCEL THE SHOOTING...
...I SHOULD AT LEAST...
uh huh!
...ASK FOR A BREAK...
UM...
DIRECTOR, IT'S NO GOOD.

YUMIKO'S COMPLETELY FALLEN INTO A HOLE.
She's in a panic.
HMM.
SHOULD WE LET HER TAKE A BREAK ...?
We really don't have time for that.
!!
phew
GOOD...
NO, DIRECTOR.
?!
HUH?!
IF WE TAKE A BREAK, WE CAN'T FINISH THE SHOOTING ON SCHEDULE.
LET'S CONTINUE.
M-MR. TSURUGA!
YOU! YOU'RE THE ONE WHO NEEDS TO TAKE A BREAK THE MOST!
BUT YUMIKO...
Why do I mess up? I can't do it. I'm afraid of saying my lines!
SHE'S ALL RIGHT.
SHE'LL DO IT THE NEXT TIME.
UM...

MR. TSURUGA!
Hey!
YUMI-KO.
IT'S ALL RIGHT. CALM DOWN.
SAY "SUS-PENDED" TEN TIMES.
SUSPENDED?
YES, SUS-PENDED.
SUS-PENDED SUS-PENDED SUS-PENDED SUS-PENDED SUS-PENDED SUS-PENDED ...
... SUSPENDED SUSPENDED SUSPENDED SUSPENDED.
GOOD, THEN CHANGE THE "ENDED" TO "ICIOUS".
....
SUSPICIOUS SUSPICIOUS SUSPICIOUS SUSPICIOUS SUSPICIOUS SUSPICIOUS SUSPICIOUS SUSPICIOUS SUSPICIOUS SUSPICIOUS.
YOU'VE GOT IT.
SEE...
...IT'S NOT SO HARD.
Good job.
OK
I DID IT?!
NOW TRY SAYING YOUR LINE.
"EXTREMELY SUSPICIOUS."
OK
"EX-TREMELY SUSPI-CIOUS."
"EX-TREMELY SUSPI-CIOUS."
Oh.
SHE SAID IT.
Yeah yeah.
REN'S A REALLY NICE GUY!

IF YOUR PARTNER'S IRRITATED, YOU FEEL EVEN MORE PRES-SURED!
She's lucky she's acting with the mild-man-nered Ren!
MR. TSURUGA...
All right. Let's try it then.
Yes.
EVEN I, WHO WAS WATCHING ON THE SIDE-LINES, WAS IRRI-TATED...
So much that I got my angry spirit out.
BUT HE'S SMILING...
IF IT WERE ME, HE'D...
I'M SUR-PRISED YOU WANT TO BE AN ACTRESS... WHEN YOU CAN'T EVEN SAY THAT LINE PROP-ERLY...
sigh
Oh... my head hurts...
WHY DON'T YOU QUIT?
You're being a pain.
... SAY...
...SOME-THING LIKE THAT FOR SURE!

......
HMPH...
HE IS...
...NICE TO EVERY-ONE BUT ME...
OF COURSE...
...ORDINARY PEOPLE WHO JOIN SHOW-BIZ...
...HAVE NO REASON TO BE DISLIKED BY MR. TSURUGA.
BECAUSE THEY SIMPLY WANT TO BRING OUT THEIR BEST IN SHOW-BIZ.
hmph
All right. Let's pull ourselves together. Standby!
Yes!
heh heh heh
EVEN IF YOU SEARCH ALL OVER THE WORLD...
...I'M ABOUT THE ONLY WOMAN THAT MR. TSURUGA DISLIKES.
IT'S ALL RIGHT. THAT'S FINE WITH ME.
zssh
Yes, I think I was at fault...
AT THIS POINT, I NEVER WANT ANYBODY TO LIKE ME AS LONG AS I LIVE!
Espe-cially MEN!
...But I just don't under-stand!
BECAUSE...
Because there's something wrong with that person.

... I'M ...
...LIVING FOR REVENGE!
WARRGH!
Shotarooooo, until I crush him with my hands, I can't die even if I WANT to!
...it's ex-tremely suspi-cious!
Blah
chank
vrr
chank
chank
GOOD, HURRY UP! DIS-MANTLE THINGS QUICKLY!
Yes!
clank
clank
Blah
Blah
HEY, CLEAN UP MORE OVER THERE! WE DON'T WANT COM-PLAINTS!
OH. WHERE'S REN AND YUMI-KO?
I THINK THEY'RE IN THEIR REHEARSAL ROOMS GETTING READY TO MOVE.
GOOD. YOU GO HELP REN.
HUH?
WELL...I CAN'T JUST DEPEND ON THAT SUBSTITUTE MANAGER GIRL.
Ah ha ha ha.
HE'S ALL RIGHT.
HE'S TSURUGA!

...
TSURU-
GA...

EVEN IF THAT DAIMANE GIRL IS NO GOOD...

...WILL BE ABLE TO TAKE CARE OF HIMSELF JUST FIIIINE!

First Rehearsal Room

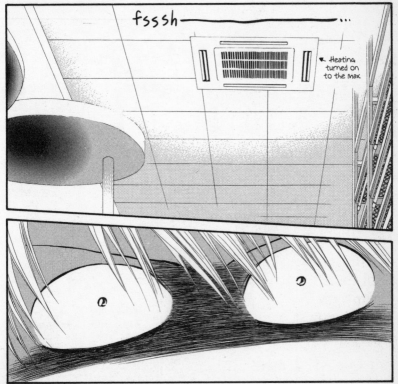

fsssh

← Heating turned on to the max

UH... UM...
...WH-WHAT SHOULD I DO?
PASSED OUT
FROZEN
Both of them can't do anything anyhow.

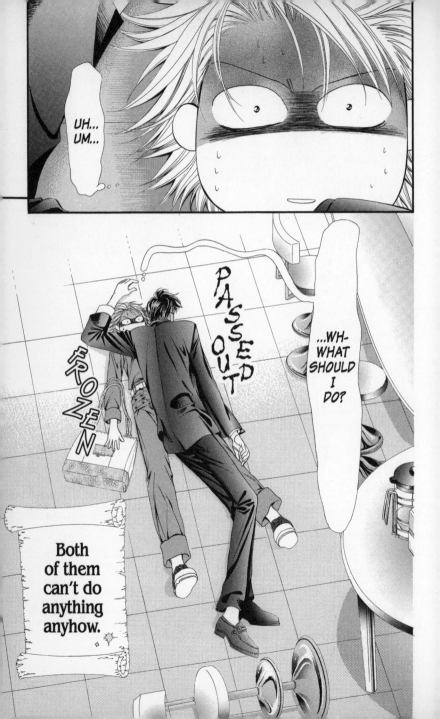

MAYBE HE'S ALREADY LOST CONSCIOUSNESS?!

Oh, no!

MR. TSU-RU-GA!

M-MR. TSU-RU-GA.

shake shake

WAKE UP, PLEASE!

shiver shiver

HE'S SHIVERING... HIS FEVER HAS RISEN...

!

oh!

sa

Wow, he's really feverish.

wriggle wriggle urmph urmph urmph wonk wonk

mph mph

urg urg

I-I'VE GOT TO ESCAPE FROM UNDER MR. TSURUGA.

Otherwise I can't do anything.

Ahh!

WH-WHAT SHOULD I DO?

wheeze wheeze wheeze wheeze
Pant pant Pant pant
EXHAUSTED
I FEEL LIKE I'M A BUG...
Blah Blah
YES YES. WHAT? YOU THINK SO TOO?
Eeeee!
huh?
OH, THAT VOICE...
...from next door...
YUMIKO!
HOW CAN YOU TALK ON THE PHONE SO MERRILY?!
twitch
twitch twitch twitch
BECAUSE OF ALL YOUR OUTTAKES...
...THINGS ARE REALLY SERIOUS HERE RIGHT NOW!
YES, IF THERE WEREN'T ANY OUTTAKES, THIS WOULDN'T HAVE HAPPENED!
twitch twitch
AH... THINKING ABOUT IT IS TICKING ME OFF EVEN MORE...
EVEN I CAN SAY THAT LINE SMOOTHLY.
"YES, I THINK I WAS AT FAULT."
Right?
"BUT I JUST DON'T UNDERSTAND!"
Perk

fu
"BECAUSE THERE'S SOMETHING WRONG WITH THAT PERSON."
IT'S EX-TREMELY SUSPI-CIOUS!"
THAT'S WHY...
...I'M TELLING YOU NOT TO ACT HASTILY...

HUH?
NO ONE...

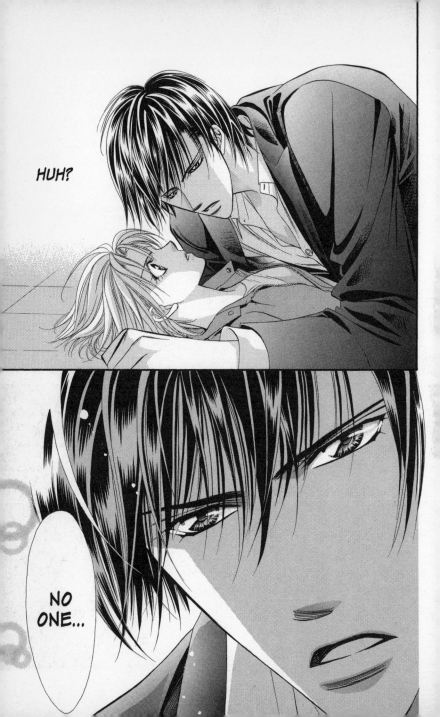

...CAN ESCAPE ...
...FROM ME...

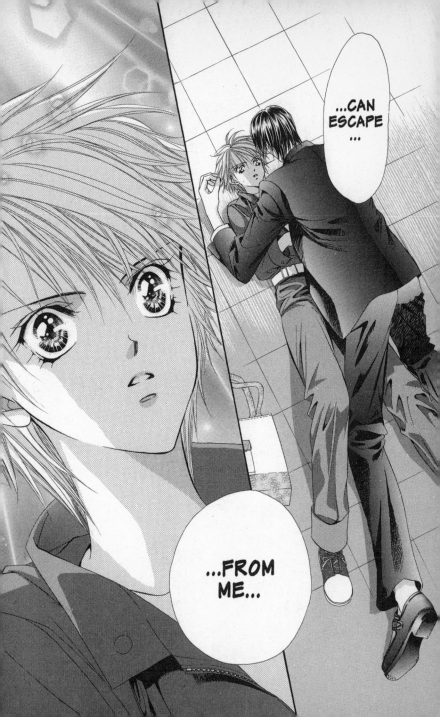

oh!
HUH?
stare
YOU'RE NOT YUMI-KO...
What're you doing here?
whump
...
H...

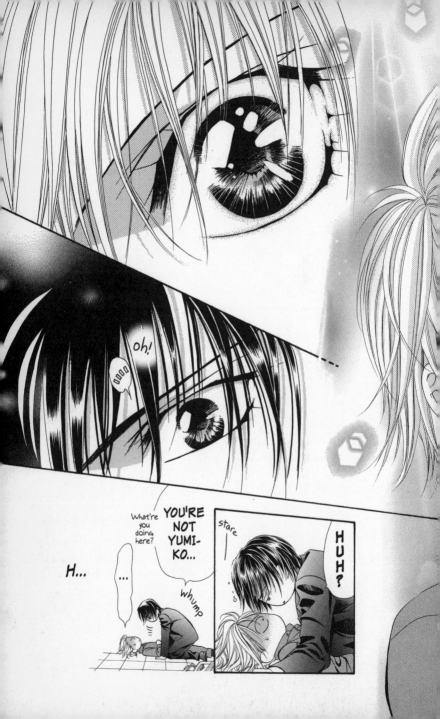

He surprised me!
He surprised me!
HE SURPRISED ME!
Th-thump
Th-thump
Th-thump
Th-thump
Th-thump
CUZ THE GUY WHO PASSED OUT SUDDENLY RESPONDED WITH HIS LINE!
Huh?
I was unconscious? Me?
Why?
Out of it
AND WHEN I LOOKED IN HIS EYES, HE WAS COMPLETELY IN HIS ROLE.
WEIGHED DOWN
50 lb
meh
M-My head feels heavy...
I feel like I'm walking on air...
Wobble wobble
tottering
Why?
Your fever's rising.
Th-thump
Th-thump
Th-thump
HE'S IN THIS CONDITION...
MR. TSURUGA, THE NEXT SCENE... YOU SHOULD TAKE TODAY OFF!
50 lb
HALT
...YET HE REACTED TO A LINE IN THE DRAMA...
...AND REGAINED CONSCIOUSNESS.
THIS GUY...

"I SAID...

...THAT I'LL KEEP ACTING UNTIL I LOSE CONSCIOUS-NESS."

...WHAT A MAN!

...
REALLY LOVE...

...HE MUST...

...ACT-ING...

THAT MEANS...

HE SHUT ME UP WITH HIS GAZE...

...

Blah

Blah

Blah

...

The next shooting location

scree scree scree

hmph
fwip
DASH
Kyaaa—! Rennn—!!
Curious crowd
Rehearsal
The actual shoot
Cut, Okay!
Okay!
The shooting progressed, and it's now time for the indoor scene.
GOOD JOB, TSURUGA. HERE'S YOUR LUNCH.
But it's already 2.
TH...
THANK YOU.
Huh?
ISN'T YOUR VOICE A BIT HOARSE?
YES... SINCE I'VE BEEN SPEAKING A LOT...
UH OH. YOU'VE GOT TO DRINK SOMETHING.
Ah ha ha.
YES.

BY THE WAY...
I haven't seen her around.
...WHERE'S THE GIRL WHO'S YOUR DAIMANE?
YOU HAVE TO GO TO YOUR NEXT JOB, RIGHT?
.....
YES...
WELL... IF SHE DOESN'T COME BACK WHILE YOU'RE EATING, YOU SHOULD JUST LEAVE HER AND GO.
....
YES.
WELL WELL, SHE'S NO GOOD.
Is it just what the Director was afraid of?
IT MEANS SHE'S STILL JUST A KID.
She's probably goofing off some-where.
.....
Then see you!
....
....
mehh...

The Reason for Giving Up

❀❀❀ ❀❀❀ ❀❀❀

When Kyoko took care of Ren, one thing I was at a loss about was the ice BAG. Nowadays, when you have a fever, the Hiepita does the JOB. The ice BAG I know was the old model that Ren uses in the story. However, right BeFore I GOt to work, I found out that there is a newer model. I BOUGHt it, thinking "I want to use it for sure!"...I did...Buy it...But the ice BAG I so looked forward to, when it's used...

...turns into...

...a shape like this...

I hesitated putting the old model on Ren's forehead, so I leapt at the newest model... ♭ the latest ice BAG has multiple functions and is wonderful!!... B-But...with that on his forehead, Ren's smile and his lines are ruined (I...I apol-oGize 🎀 to the manufacturer!!) A-Anyway, it was fatal picture-wise (maybe it's not that BAD...? ♭)

—To Be Continued—

......

GHHH...

wheeze
wheeze

pant
pant

She's supporting him
with her head.

crink
crink

...

....

YOU...

I DIDN'T
KNOW WHAT
I WAS
GOING TO
DO IF I
COULDN'T
GET BACK
IN TIME.

sigh
pant
pant

I'M
GLAD.

...

I—

Plop

rustle

S-SHOP-PING?
She went shop-ping?
YES!
Pant
I TOLD YOU I REPORTED YOUR CONDITION TO SUPERVISOR MATSUSHIMA LAST NIGHT.
I RECEIVED A LITTLE MONEY FOR EXPENSES THEN...
VROOOOM
...SO I FIGURED I'D DO MY BEST SO THAT YOU CAN CONCENTRATE ON YOUR WORK!
?
FIRST...
rummage
rummage

rummage rummage rummage

....

AND COLD MEDI- CINE.

COUGH DROPS, COUGH SYRUP.

AND THIS IS...

AN ICE PILLOW.

AN ICE-BAG, WHICH I KNOW YOU WON'T HAVE AT YOUR PLACE.

PI!

PON——k

... HIE- PITA!

sha

Special Selection HONEY

YIKES

GRATE GRATE GRATE GRATE

DAIKON RADISH

?!

?!

gloom

clink
YOU ...
... USUALLY CUT THE DAIKON INTO SMALL CUBES.
She put in a little shaved ice, too.
BUT MR. TSURUGA...
...YOU USUALLY DON'T HAVE MUCH OF AN APPETITE...
...AND I THOUGHT IT'S HARD FOR YOU TO SWALLOW SOMETHING NOW...
.....
...SO I GRATED IT, SO IT'S EASIER TO EAT.
Here.
THIS IS...
...GOOD WHEN YOU HAVE A SORE THROAT.
HOW ...
... DOES SHE KNOW ?
.....

...THAT MY THROAT'S SO SORE I DON'T EVEN WANT TO DRINK WATER...
....
...SO I FIGURED I'D DO MY BEST SO THAT YOU CAN CONCENTRATE ON YOUR WORK...
NO, MR. TSURUGA. EVEN IF YOU DON'T WANT TO EAT ANYTHING, YOU'VE GOT TO!
OTHERWISE YOU CAN'T TAKE YOUR MEDICINE!
Yes.
And she's making some mysterious food again.
stir stir
Cooking in the car. Good boys and girls shouldn't do this.
SHE MUST HAVE HAD A REALLY HARD TIME...
99¢
...FINDING AND BUYING ALL THAT STUFF...
Since there are only office buildings around there.
I DIDN'T THINK SHE'D GO THIS FAR FOR ME.
I THOUGHT SHE ONLY DID HER BEST WHEN FUWA...
...OR HER "DEBUT" ARE INVOLVED...
munch

THIS IS GOOD...
Better than I'd expected...
I...
...WAS ABLE TO SWALLOW IT WITHOUT ANY PROBLEMS.
MR. TSURUGA...
...I'LL DO EVERYTHING I CAN DO TO SUPPORT YOU.
WHAT?
WE WON'T CANCEL ANY OF YOUR JOBS...
shake shake
...AND WE'LL CURE YOUR COLD!
IF YOU'RE ABOUT TO COLLAPSE...
...THEN...
...PLEASE LEAN ON ME AGAIN!

NOW I THINK ABOUT IT...
...SHE WAS...
... ALWAYS LIKE THIS.
HERE'S YOUR MEDICINE.
SHE WAS...
... ALWAYS DOING HER BEST...
...AT EVERYTHING...
....
MAYBE...
...I...
...OVERLOOKED SOMETHING IMPORTANT...
... BLINDED BY HER MOTIVE OF REVENGE?
HER...
...TRUE SELF!
End of Act 34

Skip·Beat!

Act 35: Dislike x Dislike

MY IMPRESSION OF HER...
...WAS OF A GIRL WHO WAS OVERLY ROMANTIC ABOUT EVERY-THING...
...WHO OFTEN CRIED ABOUT THINGS RELATED TO HER MOTHER...
...BUT...
..."SHO" MADE HER SMILE RIGHT AWAY.

SHE WAS FOUR YEARS YOUNGER THAN ME...
...BUT SHE WAS VERY PER-SEVERING...
cree
cree
...DETERMINED...
...AND...
cree
cree
...IT IMPRESSED ME HOW SHE DID HER BEST WITH EVERYTHING...
IT...
IT'S HOT...
SINCE THEN...
...MY...
Plonk
CORN. CORN!
ARE YOU ALL RIGHT?
HERE!
I wet my handkerchief.
...IMAGE OF A JAPANESE GIRL...
YOU ALL RIGHT?

icy

huh?

....

...BECAME "HER"...

OH.

I'M SORRY...

...DID I WAKE YOU UP?

164

Continued

...But it makes you laugh more than the old model... ⁶⁶ no... that's what I think... But...s-so I intended to write what shape the latest ice Bag is like, and what sort of joke I made the moment I saw it, But I don't want the readers to laugh every time they see that scene (Because I don't want people to laugh at the scene. ⌐) So I won't write aBout it...I-I'm sorry... In the maga-zine, I said I might write the reason why...

...By the way, when I was drawing, I felt that you wouldn't use ice Bags nowa-days. But, using a Hiepita would have Been dull...and she wouldn't have stayed up all night taking care of Ren...that's why I used the ice BAG, But now that I think about it, I'd forgotten the easy method of wetting a towel with ice water... ⌐ That would have Been even more like taking care of Ren without any sleep!!...why didn't I think of it...it pains me...

...SO PLEASE GO BACK TO SLEEP.

I...

...JUST CHANGED THE ICE...

.....

G-OOD.

Yes.

IT FEELS GOOD...

... KS.

WHAT?

....

sha

THIS SHOULD LAST UNTIL THE MORN-ING.

THANKS...
Smile
...KYOKO.

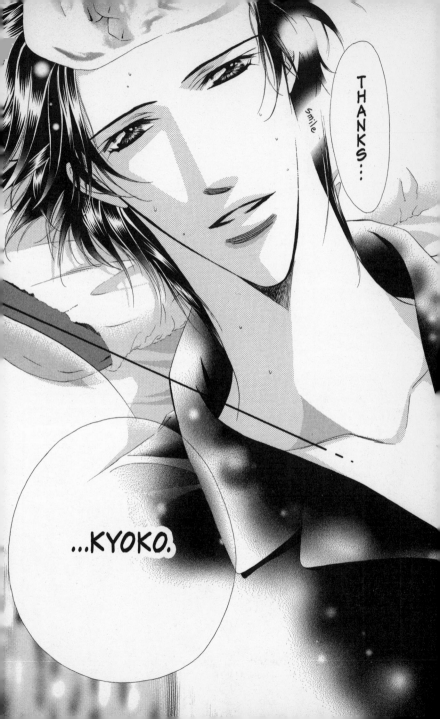

oh!
chirp
chirp chirp
chirp
UH...
...WHAT?
chirp chirp
IT...
IT'S MORNING?!
06:05
NO!
I...
...HAVEN'T SOLVED A SINGLE PROBLEM ALL NIGHT!
SH~~OCK
She opened the book of drills and simply sat there.
And...
...SINCE THEN.
...KYOKO.
WHAT?!
SNAP

...I... AM...
A...
....
...DISTURBED?!
It can't be!
HE WAS JUST TALKING IN HIS SLEEP.
HE MUST HAVE THOUGHT I WAS SOME-BODY ELSE!
THERE ARE ENOUGH WOMEN IN JAPAN WITH THE NAME "KYOKO"!
HIS FEVER WAS OVER 102 F.
He doesn't know whether he's dreaming or whether he's awake.
OR...
...MR. TSURUGA WOULDN'T CALL ME "KYOKO"!
HE'S NEVER EVEN CALLED ME BY MY LAST NAME.
AND HE STARTED TO DISLIKE ME THE SECOND TIME WE MET.
mumble mumble
stitch stitch
She's making clothes for her curse dolls to calm down.
MR. TSURU-GA...
...CALL-ING MY NAME...
...WITH SUCH A SOFT EXPRES-SION...
...AND A SOFT VOICE...
...UN-LESS...
...I GIVE UP ON HAVING MY REVENGE AGAINST SHOTARO...

... THERE'S NO WAY THAT WOULD HAPPEN ...
I can't... give up...
...I'm living to drag Shotaro into Hell.
IT'S ...
...ALL RIGHT.
I...
... DON'T ...
...WANT HIM TO CALL MY NAME SOFTLY...
MMM?
chirp chirp
chirp chirp
......
......
chirp chirp
chirp chirp
IT'S MORNING?

WHAT TIME IS IT?
slosh
sha
....
He's wearing his PJs.
....
ICE BAG
slosh
....
slosh
slosh
ICE PILLOW
...Huh?
...
Chak
I... DON'T QUITE UNDER-STAND WHAT'S HAPPENED ...
...BUT I FEEL MUCH BETTER ...
tmp
tmp
tmp

....
.....
Math
......
High School Entrance Exams
Science
English
English for Idiots
vrrr
vrrr
I SEE...
...I understand now...
noteBook
vrrr vrrr vrrr
....
UM...
vrrr
vrr
vrr
vrr
vrr
1852 FRANCE. NAPOLEON III TAKES THE THRONE.
1853. THE CRIMEAN WAR.
froth froth
1865 RUSSIA. EMANCIPATION OF THE SERFS.
1887. GERMAN-RUSSIAN SECURITY PACT.
mumble mumble
1890.
mumble mumble
mumble mumble
vrr vrr vrr vrr
Bubble Bubble Bubble
Bubble Bubble
GIOP
Blurp Blurp Blurp
GIOP
1891...
mumble mumble

EXCUSE ME...
...MYSTERIOUS OBJECTS ARE TURNING INTO EVEN MORE MYSTERIOUS OBJECTS HERE AND THERE.
WHAT?!
Oh, Mr. Tsuruga...
HUH?!
glurp glurp
Scortch scortch
Kyaaa!
Oh no! What happened?! How did this happen?!
I...
I'M SORRY...
GLOOM
I BORROWED YOUR KITCHEN WITHOUT PERMISSION...
...AND I COULD ONLY MAKE TYPICAL THINGS LIKE THIS.
Plum-flavored rice gruel
Vegetable soup
NO...
...I THINK THIS IS PRETTY RARE...
IT'S A STAMINA JUICE. ONE SIP AND YOU CAN ENJOY IT MANY TIMES.
Amazing color
HMM.
klonk
YOU LIED...
SCARY...
I was duped...
I...
crack
grip

I said you can "enjoy" it, but I didn't mean the taste!
Look at the color! Did you really think it'd taste good?!
BUT...IF IT WAS THIS DEATHLY, I WANTED YOU TO TELL ME FIRST.
I was dizzy for a moment.
AND YOU DIDN'T EVEN WARN ME.
DO YOU ...
...HATE ME THAT MUCH?
....
beep beep
beep beep
beep beep
Sound of the thermometer
oh!
oh!
100 F.
It...
...HAS GONE DOWN QUITE A BIT.

IT'S ALL THANKS TO YOU.
THANKS.
THE SHOT AT THE HOSPITAL TO BRING DOWN YOUR FEVER WORKED.
So your fever should've gone down by morning.
BUT...
...YOU PREPARED THE ICE PILLOW AND THE ICE BAG, RIGHT?
!!
NO!
DOES MR. TSURUGA REMEMBER?!
KYOKO...
AND...
...YOU EVEN CHANGED MY CLOTHES.
When I imagine myself being changed from top to bottom by a young girl...
YOU CHANGED BY YOURSELF!
You have nothing to be embarrassed about!
He's a little embarrassed...
She's a little embarrassed, too.
MR. TSURUGA, PLEASE!
His consciousness.
YOU HAVE TO OPEN THE DOOR TO THE APARTMENT FOR ME!
wobble wobble
"BECAUSE THERE'S SOMETHING WRONG WITH THAT PERSON. IT'S EXTREMELY SUSPICIOUS."
huh?
sproing
"THAT'S WHY... ...I'M TELLING YOU NOT TO ACT HASTILY."
Now!
"MR. TSURUGA, OPEN THE DOOR!"
She's talking as if she's saying her lines.
Yes.
"ALL RIGHT."
She had him change the same way, too.
I'M NOT SURPRISED YOU DON'T REMEMBER.
I'VE NEVER EVEN UNDRESSED SHOTARO... I WOULDN'T BE ABLE TO DO SUCH A BOLD THING...

ANYWAY, MR. TSURUGA ...
...IF YOU FIND IT HARD TO EAT, PLEASE AT LEAST DRINK THE SOUP.
I'm done.
Ren asked her to, so they ate together.
bow
EX-CUSE ME...
...I'LL COOK SOME-THING...
...THAT WE CAN TAKE WITH US.
....
DO YOU...
...HATE ME THAT MUCH?
IT...
...WAS A JOKE...
I made her freeze up.
WELL... I'VE ONLY DONE THINGS THAT'D MAKE HER HATE ME.
So of course she would.
clink

...
gulp
...THIS IS GOOD... SURPRISINGLY...
REALLY ...
SIGH—...
slump
BUT ...
SHE PROBABLY THINKS THAT NO MATTER HOW MUCH SHE TRIES, THAT I'D NEVER GIVE HER A "FULL MARKS" STAMP...
.....
Sheesh...
...she's so stubborn...
WHY WOULD ...
... SHE TRY ...
...I'LL DO EVERYTHING I CAN DO TO SUPPORT YOU.
IF...
...YOU'RE ABOUT TO COLLAPSE ...
shake shake
WE WON'T CANCEL ANY OF YOUR JOBS...
...AND WE'LL CURE YOUR COLD!
...SO HARD FOR SOMEONE SHE HATES?
...THEN PLEASE LEAN ON ME AGAIN!
REALLY...

SHE HASN'T CHANGED AT ALL...
3 PM
All right, cut!
Okay!
Blah Blah
!!
huh?
OH NO, I WATCHED THE SCENE AGAIN!
She had it open uselessly.
WHEN MR. TSURUGA IS ACTING, I CAN'T HELP WATCHING HIM!
CUZ I CAN LEARN FROM IT...
ANNOYED
GRR GRR
He always gets in my way!
rum-mage
I'LL CHANGE THE SUBJECT AND GIVE MYSELF A BREAK.

Kiichi: (sullenly) You really hate me, right..."
shup
Forest of Spirals last episode
OH.
MR. TSURUGA RECEIVED IT YESTERDAY, AND I'M TAKING CARE OF IT.
flip flip flip flip
Forest of Spirals last episode
Produced/Copyrighted by TBM
HE HAS TO MEMORIZE HIS LINES BY TOMOR-ROW...
...But he was in no condition to do anything yesterday...
Hmm?
WHAT IS THIS? THIS IS JUST LIKE WHAT MR. TSURUGA SAID THIS MORNING!
Bwa ha ha ha!
They're checking the monitor.
HA!
DO YOU...
...HATE ME THAT MUCH?
.....
Forest

OF COURSE ...
...I'M NOT GENEROUS ENOUGH TO LIKE SOMEONE WHO DOESN'T LIKE ME.
reading
YET...
...I COULDN'T ANSWER HIM FOR A MOMENT.
I DIDN'T KNOW HOW TO ANSWER HIM.
...MAKING HIM FOOD...
...YOU'RE GENEROUS ENOUGH.
fwip fwip
The Ren curse doll
The mean version
NO NO...
... TAKING CARE OF SOMEONE YOU HATE ALL EVEN-ING...
YOU'RE ...
Ventrilo-quism
...REALLY STUPID, AREN'T YOU?
...
ARE YOU MIMICK-ING ME?
shake shake
shake shake

Gentle-manly
Smile
YOU'RE PRETTY GOOD.
NOOOOOO!
H-HE HEARD ME!
SECRETLY PLAYING WITH THE REN DOLL!
SHIVER
Nooooo, h-he's SMILING!
Oh.
YOU'RE WELL PREPARED. YOU GOT OUT THE SCRIPT FOR THE LAST EPISODE FOR ME.
N-NO! I HOPE HE DIDN'T SEE THE CURSE DOLL THAT RADIATES A REALLY DEPRESSING AURA!
To other people, it looks like a pretty doll.
Th-thump
Th-thump
Th-thump
Sha—aaa

Blah
Blah
What should we do during break?
Let's go to the café down-stairs.
OH?
fwip fwip
flip
....
...
DARN...
...I CAN'T LEARN IT AT ALL...
Ugh...
...MY FEVER'S RISING AGAIN.
HUH?
SHE...
How well-timed.
.....
Kiichi: (sullenly) You really hate me, right..."

...JUST HAPPENS TO DO HER BEST FOR ME, WHOM SHE HATES.
mumble mumble
You're really stupid, aren't you?
She called herself stupid, so she must realize she is.
...SHE MUST LOSE HERSELF AND DEVOTE HERSELF TOWARDS FUWA...
THE SAME WAY...
NOW I REMEMBER... THAT THE MORE SHE HATED SOMETHING, THE MORE ABNORMALLY SHE FOUGHT AGAINST IT.
I HATE STUDYING!
BUT I'LL GET A 100% THE NEXT TIME FOR SURE!
And I'm gonna have Mother compliment me!
YEAH!
REVENGE SPIRIT
WELL... ...THAT'S GOOD IN A WAY...
Because you'll get better at things you're not good at.
And it's good for your sake, too.
BUT...
...ABOUT FUWA...
...WHAT'LL SHE GAIN BY HAVING HER REVENGE?

THERE HE IS!

...BUT WAS FOR HER-SELF...

...I'D BE...

FOR EXAMPLE, IF STUDYING ACTING...

...WASN'T PART OF HER PLAN FOR REVENGE AGAINST FUWA...

SHE SHOULD USE HER TIME FOR HERSELF MORE...

Oh.

tmp

Uh...

No... I won't think about it anymore.

A LITTLE MORE?

WHAT?

....

...A LITTLE MORE...

I HAVE MORE IMPORTANT THINGS TO...

...SO I FIGURED HE WAS READING IT WHERE THERE'S NO ONE AROUND.

dash

THE SCRIPT WAS GONE...

MR. TSU-RU-GA!

HE HAS TO TAKE LIQUIDS DURING THE BREAK!
Apple juice
Ginger tea
Syrup drink
MR...
"48 HOURS UNTIL THE STATUTE OF LIMITATIONS TAKES EFFECT."
mumble mumble
H-HIS LINES!
mumble mumble mumble mumble
SHWIP
Oh!
I- I DON'T HAVE TO HIDE FROM HIM, DO I?!
NO...
... BUT...
...S- SOME-HOW...
mumble mumble
mumble mumble mumble mumble
...I FELT THAT I HEARD SOMETHING THAT I SHOULDN'T HAVE!
MR. TSURUGA DOESN'T USUALLY LEARN HIS LINES BY SAYING THEM OUT LOUD...
MAYBE...
Investi-gated by private detective Kyoko
...HE'S HAVING TROUBLE LEARN-ING THEM?
"48 HOURS UNTIL THE STATUTE OF LIMITATIONS TAKES EFFECT."
mumble mumble
OH.
HE'S SAYING THOSE LINES AGAIN ...

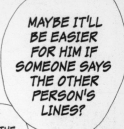

MAYBE IT'LL BE EASIER FOR HIM IF SOMEONE SAYS THE OTHER PERSON'S LINES?
"IF THE PREFECTURAL POLICE IS GOING TO INVESTIGATE..."
AFTER MR. TSURUGA'S LINE HERE, THE NEXT LINE WAS...
"ARE YOU GOING TO RUN AWAY?"
"...WE CAN'T DO ANYTHING ANYMORE."
Forest of Spirals
last episode
"YOUR KILLER LINE MAKES ME LAUGH."
!!

HER VOICE ...
...from Below?
"YAZAKI IS THE ENEMY WHO KILLED YOUR FATHER!
YOU'VE HATED HIM FOR 15 YEARS!"
...
"IF YOU'RE NOT GOING TO ARREST HIM, WHO WILL?!"
HER SPEAKING...
"DON'T YOU GET ANGRY."
A LINE WHERE'S SHE'S ANGRY.
...HER BREATHING...
"I'M THE ONE WHO'S PISSED THAT THE PREFECTURAL POLICE TOOK YAZAKI AWAY."
"SO!
THEY'RE PERFECT...
THE PREFECTURAL POLICE TOOK YAZAKI ON A SEPARATE CHARGE, SO IT'S ALL RIGHT!"
tak
tak
tak
Forest of Spirals last episode
I'M SURPRISED ...
"WE'LL GET HIM ON THE ROBBERY AND MURDER, FOR WHICH THE STATUTE OF LIMITATIONS IS ABOUT TO EXPIRE!"
WHEN DID SHE JOIN THE TRAINING SCHOOL?

tmp
THIS...
...IS...
...AN AMATEUR...
...WHO'S BEEN STUDYING ACTING FOR LESS THAN SIX MONTHS?
...
"DO YOU INTEND TO BEAT...
...THE PREFEC-TURAL POLICE?"

grin
THIS IS...

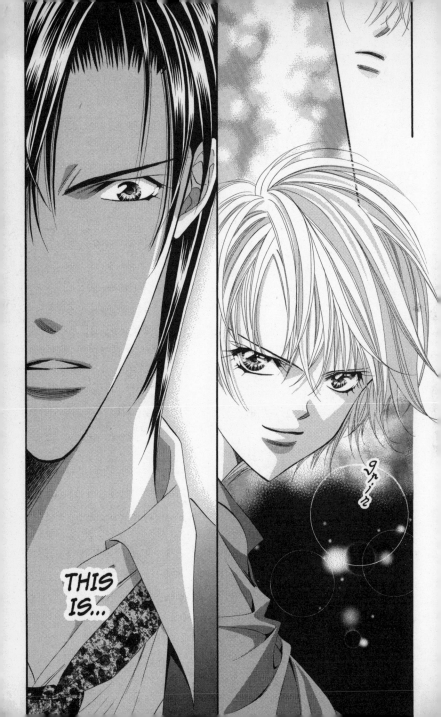

"OF COURSE..."

...WHAT SHE'S LEARNED...

...ONLY...

...FOR REVENGE?!

End of Act 35

Skip·Beat! End Notes
Everyone knows how to be a fan, but sometimes cool things
from other cultures need a little help crossing the language barrier.

Page 13, sidebar: Yanki
A slang term for teen gangs of delinquents, bikers and dropouts. The word
probably originates from the American "Yankee" GIs, who brought their
love of rock 'n' roll and rebellion to Japan.

Page 57, panel 3-4: Not attending school
Unlike in the U.S., compulsory education in Japan stops at middle school.
Students are not required to go to high school, although it is still socially
encouraged.

Page 63, panel 6: Daimane
Short for *dairi manager*, or substitute manager.

Page 87, panel 1: Hamburger steak
Japanese hamburgers are closer to Salisbury steak or meatloaf than the
hamburgers Americans are used to. The ground meat is mixed with bread
crumbs, egg, sautéed onions and soy sauce and served on a plate rather
than a bun. Sometimes the hamburger is topped with a fried egg.

Page 91, panel 2: My life was totally dark
This is probably a parody of the hit song by Keiko Fuji (mother of pop
singer Hikaru Utada), which goes "When I was 15, 16, 17 my life was
gloomy."

Page 132, panel 3: Spacicicious
The original Japanese phrase is *Fushin kiwaramai naiwa*, which means "It
is extremely suspicious." Yumiko pronounces it *Fushin kimawari naiwa* in
Japanese.

Page 153, sidebar: Hiepita
A cooling gel pack used to reduce the effects of a fever.

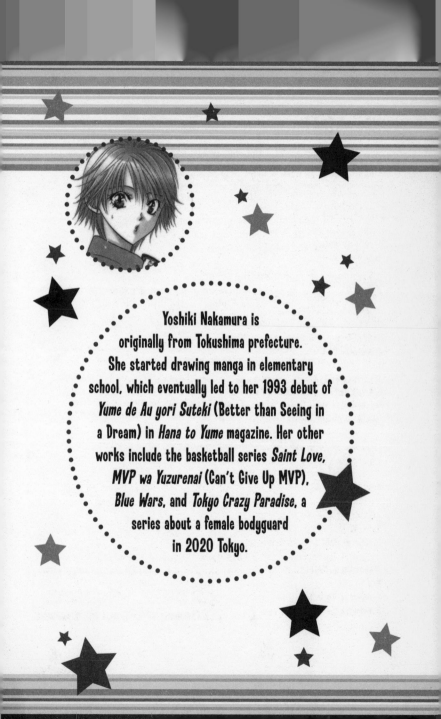

Yoshiki Nakamura is originally from Tokushima prefecture. She started drawing manga in elementary school, which eventually led to her 1993 debut of *Yume de Au yori Suteki* (Better than Seeing in a Dream) in *Hana to Yume* magazine. Her other works include the basketball series *Saint Love*, *MVP wa Yuzurenai* (Can't Give Up MVP), *Blue Wars*, and *Tokyo Crazy Paradise*, a series about a female bodyguard in 2020 Tokyo.

SKIP·BEAT!
Vol. 6
The Shojo Beat Manga Edition

STORY AND ART BY YOSHIKI NAKAMURA

English Translation & Adaptation/Tomo Kimura
Touch-up Art & Lettering/Sabrina Heep
Design/Yukiko Whitley
Editor/Pancha Diaz

Editor in Chief, Books/Alvin Lu
Editor in Chief, Magazines/Marc Weidenbaum
VP of Publishing Licensing/Rika Inouye
VP of Sales/Gonzalo Ferreyra
Sr. VP of Marketing/Liza Coppola
Publisher/Hyoe Narita

Printed in Canada

Published by VIZ Media, LLC
P.O. Box 77010
San Francisco, CA 94107

store.viz.com

Shojo Beat Manga Edition
10 9 8 7 6 5 4 3
First printing, May 2007
Third printing, February 2008

RATED T FOR TEEN

PARENTAL ADVISORY
SKIP·BEAT! is rated T for Teen and is recommended for ages 13 and up. This volume contains suggestive themes.

ratings.viz.com

I•O•N
By Arina Tanemura,
creator of *Full Moon* and *The Gentlemen's Alliance †*
Shojo Beat Manga
I•O•N
Arina Tanemura
Ion Tsuburagi is a normal junior high girl with normal junior high problems. But when a mysterious substance grants her telekinetic powers, she finds herself struggling to keep everything together! Are her new abilities a blessing...or a curse?
Find out in *I•O•N*—manga on sale now!
Shojo Beat
MANGA from the HEART
On sale at www.shojobeat.com
Also available at your local bookstore and comic store.
I•O•N © 1997 by Arina Tanemura/SHUEISHA Inc.
RATED T FOR TEEN
ratings.viz.com
VIZ media
www.viz.com

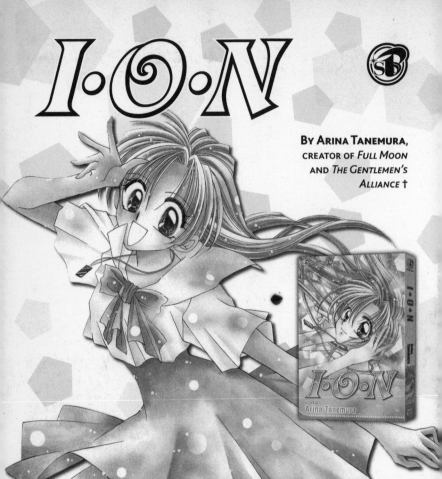

The gripping story — in manga format
Shojo Beat Manga
Be With You
Be With You
Sai Kawashima
Takuji Ichikawa
Yoko Iino
Written by
Takuji Ichikawa
Art by
Sai Kawashima
Script by
Yoko Iino
Complete in one volume!
Get the complete Be With You collection—
buy the manga and fiction today!
Ima Ainiyukimasu © Sai KAWASHIMA, Takuji ICHIKAWA, Yoko IINO/Shogakukan Inc.
Ima Ainiyukimasu © Takuji ICHIKAWA/Shogakukan Inc.
RATED
T
FOR
TEEN
ratings.viz.com
viz media
www.viz.com

Be With You
Is it possible to experience first love
for a second time?
The answer, as Be With You
proves, is yes—
a million times yes
Be With You
Takuji Ichikawa
TRANSLATED BY TERRY GALLAGHER
TAKUJI ICHIKAWA
The hit novel that inspired the manga series
SB FICTION
Shojo Beat
MANGA from the HEART
On sale at:
www.shojobeat.com
Also available at your local bookstore and comic store.

Tell us what about Shojo Beat Manga!

Our survey is now available online. Go to:

shojobeat.com/mangasurvey

Help us make our product offerings better!

Shojo Beat™

MANGA from the HEART

The Shojo Manga Authority

12 GIANT issues for ONLY $34.99*

That's 51% OFF the cover price!

The most **ADDICTIVE** shojo manga stories from Japan **PLUS** unique editorial coverage on the arts, music, culture, fashion, and much more!

Subscribe NOW and become a member of the ⑤ᵇ Sub Club!

- **SAVE** 51% OFF the cover price
- **ALWAYS** get every issue
- **ACCESS** exclusive areas of www.shojobeat.com
- **FREE** members-only gifts several times a year

Strictly VIP!

3 EASY WAYS TO SUBSCRIBE!

1) Send in the subscription order form from this book **OR**
2) Log on to: www.shojobeat.com **OR**
3) Call 1-800-541-7876

www.viz.com